JOURNEY INTO THE EYE OF A NEEDLE

Journey into the Eye
of a Needle

Maurice Ash

GREEN BOOKS

First published in 1989 by
Green Books
Ford House, Hartland
Bideford, Devon EX39 6EE

© Maurice Ash, 1989

Typeset by
Fine Line Publishing Services
Witney, Oxon

Printed on recycled paper by
Hartnolls, Victoria Square
Bodmin, Cornwall

British Library Cataloguing in Publication Data
Ash, Maurice 1917 -
  Journey into the Eye of a Needle
  1. Environment, Effects on man
  I. Title
  304.2

ISBN 1-870098-35-8

I have a journey, Sire, shortly to go.
My master calls me; I cannot say no.

To the memory of
Dorothy Whitney Elmhirst

Acknowledgement

M Y THANKS go to Stephen Batchelor, who as editor of this book forced me time and again to make more intelligible for public reading what had initially been intended only for private reference.

Conventionally, I suppose, one should then go on to say that responsiblity for the views expressed are one's own alone, but in this case I am not so sure. In particular, I still don't know whether remarks touching on the distinction between belief and faith are his or mine. All I can say is that the discussion between us continues.

Foreword

W HAT DOES IT MEAN to set out on a 'journey into the eye of a needle'? Has this not been taught to be a hopeless endeavour? I suspect that the author of this book would reply that it is the only option that remains open to us now. For Maurice Ash is keenly aware of the impasse at which our pampered Western civilisation has arrived. And is this impasse not comparable to that biblical needle's eye?

This book is a book of exploration, a journey into a rarely visited land. For such journeys no neatly charted maps exist. True, people have been there before, but have returned with accounts that are often at odds with each other. How frustrating this is for a reader of travelogues! How can it be, we ask ourselves in frustration, that this person saw a mountain where the other saw a lake? Surely there must be either one or the other. Both cannot stand in one place.

The journey recounted here begins and ends with the same teasing question: What is the meaning of a life? In the very last chapter we are told that this means no more than: Why do we ask this question? For all such questions are the articulations of a mystery. But because no rational solution exists, are such questions meaningless? No. If anything, they are the only ones worth asking. For it is such questions that give us the courage to undertake those journeys into the eyes of needles and storms.

On such uncharted journeys the traveller wanders hither and thither, exploring a valley here, a pass there, stumbling upon unsought for treasures, encountering unforeseen obstacles. After many surprises and much backtracking, he gains a sense of the lay of the land. But how difficult it is for him to describe to others what he has seen. There is no starting point or end point to his discovery. He has built up his understanding through trial and error. As with the Australian aborigine, he might prefer to sing his landscape than to draw a map.

Maurice Ash describes his territory as a 'maze' and his journey as the 'unstructured wandering' of his mind. But he also speaks of new 'paradigms' or 'patterns to which to conform', even 'agendas for a thousand years'. And although he sees all this as a kind of 'game' with language, he also recognises that games are played by rules, that life is lived not randomly but according to the 'forms' it assumes.

This is a journey in which we spend as much time retracing our steps as we do exploring new frontiers. For we need to know where we have been in order to understand why we are here; and we need to know what we have made of our lives in order to imagine a change. Christianity, rational knowledge and science are the places to which we need to return to uncover the past that still determines, perhaps more powerfully than we are prepared to admit, our present. St Paul, St Augustine, Hobbes, Descartes, Newton: these are some of the junctions of Western civilisation at which we must pause and reflect.

And as we stumble forward, we may find glimpses of inspiration from Blake or Tolstoy, from Nagarjuna or Dogen, from Eliot or Wittgenstein. To heal our estrangement from the world, we might reconsider the meaning of 'environment'; to curb our obsession to measure things, we might contemplate the quality of life; to quieten the clamour of self-interest, we might meditate on the silence of others; to lighten the numbing effects of the nation state, we might imagine the restoration of community.

Throughout his journey Maurice Ash resists the deceptively easy route of falling back on ready-made solutions. He can draw on the insights of Zen without becoming an

advocate of Buddhism, just as he can admire the crafts-
manship of the Shakers without espousing their Christian beliefs. The present crisis of humankind is too dire
and complex to admit of the simpler answers to the simpler problems of the past. A global crisis requires a global
solution, not an Eastern or a Western one. The immensity
of this task is as daunting as that which must have faced
the first explorers who confronted the heart of darkness in
the African interior. The thoughts of three score years and
ten, condensed into this volume, are Maurice Ash's
encounter with this immensity. Just let the words reach
beyond themselves to the 'silence of all that is speechless'.

Stephen Batchelor
Sharpham, 1989

Introduction

I F THESE PAGES should be found published within covers, it will not be because I have written a book. It will be because putting covers around words — instead of speaking them — has, all but unawares, become the accepted way of purveying 'truth'. This is the way words have come to be weighed and judged, as though they were measurable quantities. Yet it is not so long ago that there still were Celts who would not allow their legends to be stolen from them and then petrified by transcription. I have nothing as precious as that to save from atrophy; but nor, I trust, do my thoughts have all the hollow portentiousness of a book. I think I am at least aware of the pervading impermanence which the written word disguises, and in disguising desanctifies our mundane relationships. In Homeric Greece the temple and the market were necessarily one. Today, how ever, we are in an ironic situation — itself the product of too many books — in which one may be reduced to talking to oneself. And just as art in our times has to borrow devalued language to say, as the painter Francis Bacon does, that we and art itself are sick (or, as with the Mafia, the only honesty is dishonesty), so it might be legitimate to borrow the form of a book to communicate these intimate thoughts.

In writing this introduction, I had first wanted to leave it more or less at that. These meditations were compiled over a span of some ten years — a span encompassing the illness and death of my wife — and mostly written in places as far away as out of mind: Sirmione, Antibes, Montserrat, Paihia, Cephalonia. I thought that each meditation, if anyone else ever came to read it, would either speak for itself or not at all. Yet taken together they have now brought me to a point at which I doubt if I shall continue with this exercise. As I look back at them (a questionable advantage of the written word), I think they may justify a book, even if only a book of errors; for I have made a journey that I suspect many, perhaps multitudes, will soon have to take in their own way. At least it may be of interest to see where I have stumbled as I went.

The theme of this journey of re-orientation bears upon the compact St Augustine made with Rome, of which we are the heirs. It was a fatal conjunction: a compact made between an empire in breakdown and a church in rejection of its origins. Their need of one another could only be measured by the sum of their differences, manifest in an ever widening chasm between inward and outward worlds. No one should be sceptical that, a millenium and a half later, such a flawed compact could still govern our lives as it does. Just consider that admittedly lesser schism between Saxon and Norman, which the history of England papers over, but which is so much deeper in the swell of history than any of the overt 'class distinctions' that bedevil this country. The price paid by Western civilisation for the compact between St Augustine and Rome has, at all events, put us as deeply and as long in debt as any imaginable covenant could do.

The price we pay is that of our estrangement from the world. For by this compact we are what we are, each in isolation, only as our ineradicable sin defines us. Being incorrigibly sinful, moreover, our condition is such that we must submit to be governed — no matter that those to whom we submit are as sinful as we ourselves. But we must succumb, and it is by this resignation that we are defined in a timeless purgatory.

So we are lost. That has been the price of our civilisation's compact: to be lost in the undergrowth of disjunctions between our own being and that of the world (even in such contradictions as underlie the making of this 'book'). We are caught in the vice of an irresolvable dualism, one that cynically caters for a corrupt person in an arbitrary society. Indeed, it has been the lot of the West's internecine strife to endure this dualism, even as it reached its climacteric in the Great War — to which World War II was but the coda.

In binding an irredeemable person to an unaccountable world, some kind of accommodation between them might, of course, be concocted — as indeed it has been. For instance, any such accommodation would have to place a premium on morality, on prescription, and hence on unquestionable authority, and, driven thereby to take refuge in the ideal, it would lapse into the equally illusory antinomy of realism. Just such a compact with the authority of God has indeed created a false holism, a religious corporatism, to which the only possible but logically inescapable outcome is either death in the hope of life hereafter, or nihilism. This is what happens when divine justice underpins natural laws.

Early Christianity had maintained itself separate from temporal power, duly rendering unto Caesar that which was Caesar's. In so doing, it metaphysically maintained the person as a being precisely defined by its freedom from the world and from temporal power. Those opposites at least gave some meaning to life: all too much, perhaps, insofar as the phobia of early Christianity was that of martyrdom — though martyrdom combined with a latent claim to dominion over a paradisaic world when Caesar and his gods should be no more.

But the dualism of St Augustine's compact deprived life even of this much meaning. It left a sinful (hence permanently dying) person in an arbitrary world: a self condemned to solitude because of its enslavement to passions over whose arousal in its 'disobedient member' its will was impotent — the very impotence which nevertheless continued to define that self. Nor, as I now realise, was it by coincidence that Wittgenstein began his radical *Philosophical Investigations* with a critique of that theory of language proposed at the outset of St Augustine's

3

Confessions. Nor is it by chance — indeed, it is entirely
logical — that St Augustine's theory led him to conclude
that 'it is only that which remains in being without
change that truly is' — namely, what could only be construed as 'God'. And the power of naming things, given in
Genesis by God to Adam has had incalculable ramifica-
tions in Western civilisation. It underpins our atomism,
our premise of the discreteness of objects and their sub-
stantiality; and by extension it allows of our imputations
of reality to all the panoply of metaphysics.

Our uncontrollable organ of life contradicts the notion
of being, the singularity of the self, which we have made
the corner-stone of our civilisation. This is evidenced
equally in the Jewish sense of self-contempt and of the
ineradicability of being a Jew, as what is in essence its
Christian converse, the preservation of purity as the cata-
lyst of a perfectible society. We have excluded Pan from
our cosmology — displacing him by the dying god, Adonis:
which is to say, the ideal of the self — and our very civilisation is built along this fault-line. Out of this contradic-
tion (in which, ironically, the faculty of regeneration
denies the self its immortal soul) we have engendered
only confusion: confusion in which we strive to find ourselves.

All we actually experience, however, is a loss of identity, which is not the same as losing the self, for to lose the
self one must first have found it, just as one must use
language to arrive at a recognition of its fictions. And each
in seeking an identity through membership of this or that
disparate social entity only compounds the confusions of
the human undergrowth. The self, indeed, is inherently
wayward; not even the dogma of original sin can contain
it, any more than it could soothe St Augustine's own trou-
bled sleep. Yet the butterfly in its day of life does not seek
an identity; it dances to the rhythm of chance. We ourselves have lost the art of celebrating life. We are not even
emperors without clothes: we are just the clothes.

That inexorable division of the self against the self —

4

'alienation', to use the modern term — is, in its ever-changing forms, still with us. We find it in our cities and in our work, even in my no longer knowing my cows by their names but by their numbers. These alienations are endemic to our culture, to our leisure as to our work, no matter how much our forebears, whether Protestant, Catholic or agnostic, may have thrashed around in their philosophies to escape them. In our own epoch, Hobbes' *Leviathan* echoes the theme of the alienation of human-kind 'whose natural state is Warre', prefiguring the tortuous travails of the nation state. Consequently, one has immanently the sense of spending one's life in a labyrinth. (It may help to know that I was born in the year of Passchendale [1917] and have lived my life in the twilight of the civilisation that was destroyed there.) To find my own way through the labyrinth, then, and finally to abandon the bearings of the past, I started to put down my thoughts just as they came to me, quasi-surrealistically, without any witting constraints. These thoughts, if they are to be read at all, should be taken as dreams might be, rather than pondered on — and then be discarded.

There was no seeming coherence, no predetermined thesis to this clearing out of the attic of my mind. (What you're reading now could just as well be an epilogue as an introduction.) I found myself writing about what we mean when we speak of 'a life': about knowledge, Romanticism, dualism, religion, poetry, paradigms, politics, language, God, spirit, wholeness, environment — and about how words relate to the world. There were several more such... but that's not the point. For the point is precisely that none of these were my subjects, exhaustively treated for themselves alone. (Of course, this may mean that their treatment here is often unsatisfying; but it is not really of them I am treating.) None of these subjects seems to me significant except in relation to one or more of the others, just as I cannot look at what's around me with my own eyes alone, or listen only with my own ears. Perhaps this is how philosophy might be if ever again it could be emancipated from its (still very recent) professionalisation. As Wittgenstein understood it, philosophy might then 'leave everythingasitis'.Afterall,onesaddeningaspectofourway of life, of its specialisations, is that few people any more enjoy the luxury of letting their thoughts wander very far. Literacy itself imposes an artificial solitude upon us.

In what follows, however, I have to admit one exception to this unstructured wandering of my mind. Section 13 derives from a certain specific traffic I have had with the world, albeit with a certain unique microcosm of the world: the Dartington Hall Trust. It would seem right to include this section here, as a kind of half-way house along my journey, if only to show that all the rest grew out of some kind of ground. Yet it has a deeper relevance to my theme, for it touches upon what all these reflections of mine might imply for the way we live. More than this, it also raises questions about how we could change how we live.

The question it asks in particular is whether the application of wealth can do any abiding good in the world — for Dartington has been an essay in benefaction by private wealth. Of course, this is only a particular case of the question, but a very special case. For from time immemorial it has been assumed that it is by good works that we might find our place in heaven. Yet we have also been told it would be easier for a camel to pass through the eye of a needle than for a rich man to enter heaven. Moreover examples from the Buddha to Ludwig Wittgenstein, who both felt it necessary to renounce their worldly goods in order to live meaningful lives, are historical evidence of the impediment of wealth to the pursuit of salvation. It is a perennial spiritual phenomenon.

The idle rich, of course, are always with us. And even those who retain their wealth to use it paternalistically often seem to live with an overwhelming sense of guilt. They have a consciousness of self too great to be borne. Even though driven to do good by stealth, they fear that their isolation by wealth from their fellows constitutes an

insurmountable barrier to their being taken seriously.
Maybe, then, when we are all rich (as to past generations
we might all now seem to be) this barrier of isolation will
disappear, and poverty will no longer be a criterion of
credibility. Yet, in truth, as a glance back at the decline of
Rome all too topically suggests, widespread wealth spells
only decadence.

Perhaps the secret of charity lies not in the giving, but
in the doing: in the living of the gift. After all, quantum
theory speaks to us of stranger things than camels passing through the eye of a needle. Yet who can fail to be
haunted by that Lear-like image of the foolish old Tolstoy,
his serfs liberated to participate with him in a fuller life —
in a demonstration of lived truth — driven out in sorrow
to die in the storm? Nevertheless, the case of Dartington
is of interest precisely because it does not turn its back on
the inconvenient fact of wealth. What it has done is to
question both the givers and recipients as to what 'wealth'
means, and thus change its meaning. And it is quite
arguable that such a use of wealth might be beneficial.

What this amounts to, in effect, is that fatalism —
doing nothing to change the course of events — is not the
only, or true, alternative to the frenetic activity that
stems from our dualism, from the separation of observer
and observed and the causal relationship of one separate
thing acting upon another separate thing — all of which
leads ultimately to the hypothesis of Creation by the mind
of God. Yet, in such dualistically governed activity, unless
both parts to a relationship change, nothing changes: or,
perhaps more particularly, nothing changes by design,
but only accidentally.

There is nothing new in the recognition that a cause
cannot create an effect without the effect changing the
cause. Thus, in a world of perpetual causation we live in
the midst of uncertainty. Likewise, what we call 'things'
are actually reifications, and no thing exists except by
reason of its not being another thing. Hence, the only
change within our power lies in language, whereby these

7

reifications are made; for language is the intermediary of our relationships, the changeability of change, which gains its meaning, not from anything substantial, but from its use. And silence is just language in another form, its dialectic.

The change that language enables, then, is not in specifics, not in things each separately defined, but in the climate of ideas in terms of which life is pursued. (The world, as Wittgenstein said, waxes and wanes as a whole.) It is expressed in that interdependence of relationships that we call the environment. Meditation, it follows, far from being quiescence, is, in the activity of its silence, the greatest agent of change. By annihilation of the difference between the within and the without it comes to terms with the uncertainty which is the medium wherein we pass our lives. It creates change by the dispersal of illusions — and there are enough of these to provide the business of a thousand years. The world is as it is, and to see it as such is an act of worship that is the only way of changing it.

All of this, however, is not so much the theme of what follows, as an extension of it: an extension pointing to some better way of coming to terms with the inescapable metaphysicality of language as of art. The theme itself, as I've already mentioned, is of St Augustine's compact with Rome and the maze in which it has left us. This was a truly fatal absolute dualism. Unlike that of the early Christians, or of its paler repetition with the Romantics, this compact has held us in a vice. This vice is that of the certainty which gives words the authority to describe the world in terms of substance. In the grip of this vice, both spirit and matter have conspired to forge their fortress against the changeability of the world.

Looking back over the years, it seems to me that this was the fly-bottle out of which my writing was trying to find the way. I myself do not claim to have escaped.

1

I S IT SAFE to assume that all people think they must
make sense of their lives? Not that one must make sense
of what one will do each day when one wakes from the
timeless chaos of sleep to bring some kind of order into the
daily suspension of that chaos, but to make sense of one's
life as a whole? Maybe this assumption comes only to
those seriously faced by the prospect of dying young, 'out
of their time', as the war generations were. There may be
others who proceed placidly from stage to stage, receive
their daily bread from the supermarket, spend their last
few years on the golf course or at bingo, sheltered from the
elements even into the crematorium's maw, without ever
feeling the need to question the meaning of their lives.
And they are not to be despised, for perhaps each waking
day — as Beckett's *Happy Days* celebrates — is a self-
sufficient experience. Yet a sterile one, as Beckett knew: a
life anaesthetised by living it. For it is the same person
who wakens from each nightly possession by sleep. We do
not receive a new name each day; the fiction, if such it is,
is maintained. Hence life's thread is there also, and the
question about its sense remains.

So not to make sense of one's life is only to hide from
oneself? (Even if others make sense of it for you, you still
must make sense of what they say.) No doubt many, perhaps most of us, hide from ourselves. And who knows at
what cost? And how might that cost be assessed in terms
of our separation from reality and of the illusions we
entertain? Again, it could be the case that such amnesia is
no worse, preferable perhaps, to the false pursuits of
reality by which we delude ourselves. The delusions about

9

the soul, for instance: the poison of Plato: his 'real' self, which was so easily transmuted via Christianity into the Graeco-Judaic world by St Paul's promise of salvation for 'both Jews and Greeks under the power of sin' — sinful because, under the thrall of language, 'the venom of asps is under their tongue'. Perhaps a daily dose of bingo is a necessary antidote to these prescriptions. Nonetheless, there does remain the incredible uniqueness of each one of us, even physically. And this uniqueness stands against the background of the vastness of all that is not us. This alone, surely, is enough to convince us that perforce we must make sense of our lives.

Yet I could be mistaken. This worry may just be my old-fashioned neurosis, shared by a few self-conscious others who are also obsessively concerned about the mystery in which we find ourselves. But perhaps this is a false mystery, created by our separation from the real mystery? As the Buddhists would seem to be telling us, there is only the now. All is but process, hence 'suchness', and past and future are part of the present. So golf and bingo are perhaps not trivial after all. If they only pass the time, this is but profoundly to acknowledge how time is impossible to master, and that, to appease the now, we must, as livers of lives, immolate ourselves in virtual nonsense.

If, however, it be the case that any life is but an arrestation or even a reversal of time, then surely there is all the more reason to make sense of it, and not just to take it for granted. For the now of each life is the very realisation of process — process par excellence — and, merely to be recognised as such, such process must have a pattern. The sensing of this pattern is not just for a neurotic few; for we are all born to this anxiety, And while, in Wittgenstein's terms, the sense of the world itself may be outside the world, nothing, not even golf or bingo, can anaesthetise us to the truth that to live is to have a pattern to one's life. Living itself is the process of making sense of that pattern.

2

I T MIGHT BE SUPPOSED that the need to make sense of our
lives is what religion is all about. Indeed, it would seem
to be conceived for that purpose. But that is not at all the
kind of sense I have in mind, I only have in mind what
meaning anyone's life has in its own terms.

Theoretically, the context of anyone's life is the world
at large, in all its mystery. So, without knowledge of
this context, can any sense be made of one's life? But
this would effectively amount to saying that 'sense' can
be nothing but nonsense. It is, rather, only the sense of
'a life', or the notion of it, that now concerns me. I am
certainly not concerned here with whether my life, or
yours, is somehow sacred — let alone with the holiness
of life itself. That was not at all the point of my initial
inquiry about the sense of life. Indeed, I avow an
increasing suspicion of that deepest strain of Christian
thought which, through the construct of the trinity, has
made mankind quasi-divine, hence, set apart from
the dross of the world, and with surrogated dominion
over it.

This is why I find the heretical Arianism of Isaac
Newton so fascinating. For he held to this heresy, not
only secretly, but cravenly, for fear of losing his sinecure
at Cambridge. According to the Arian heresy, the trinity
was no more than a fraud perpetrated on Christianity
by the authority of the church. And Newton must have
known, against all his inner wisdom, that he had
fashioned the tools to consummate the 'Christian' separation of man from the world. In contrition, perhaps, he
spent a full decade of his intellectual maturity in the
hopeless and near suicidal (through mercury poisoning)
practice of alchemy, seeking without finding the locked-
away spirit that animates the world. A little earlier,

Descartes, that obedient child of the church, had announced that his 'method' would make us 'the lords and masters of nature'. Newton, however, perceived that it was Descartes who was the heretic. For, by separating the living, thinking self from the world, Descartes had deprived the world of spirit, and turned it into dead matter.

Newton's life story is a terrible parable for our times, and one that the scientific community has hardly been eager to publicise since it quite recently came to light. Yet in his story are to be found the seeds of all the alienation that plagues us today. And, in reaction to it, we also find our distressed conscience about the environment — to say nothing of the pervasive trepidation that, in the face of man's hubris, nature always has the last laugh. So my talk of making sense of our lives is only modest and practical, like Newton's attempt to make sense of his. The practicality lies simply in a current and deeply unsatisfied need, which arises from the kind of world we have inherited from Newton and Descartes. This world is one of quantification, of separate things, each to be numbered, or to be fragmented so that it can be numbered: hence a world not of process but of atoms. Our unsatisfied need, then, is to discover the meaning of what we do.

It is all very well to know about something — and better still to know about everything. Ours has, indeed, been the 'age of knowledge' — albeit knowledge about things. Such knowledge has, these past few hundred years, been given primacy because it supplied the certainty mankind craved but no longer found in the arbitrary power of princes and prelates. 'Knowledge itself is power' was the substitute offered by Bacon. This is perhaps why pure knowledge rather than applied knowledge has retained such a hold over English minds, and been enshrined as an eremitic pursuit in England's ancient universities. This has allowed learning and work to belong to different social worlds, and has well suited the class structure — as well as contributing to the *folies de grandeur* of post-empire times. But, if this substitute priesthood is now looking ever more sickly, it is largely because the certainties of knowledge itself are profoundly in question.

Partly (and all credit to it) this is because the deeper that science has explored, the less firm it has found the ground beneath itself. Because Einstein himself did not want to believe this ('God', he said of quantum theory, 'does not play dice with the universe'), he represents the last in the classic line of science, not the first of the new, and certainly not the canonisation of science itself. The atom bomb is the tragic monument to the history of that line. A curious symmetry is provided here by the initial contention posited in Descartes' ontology, that God would not deceive us about the otherwise illogical gap between the self and the world. This was the same gap as that which the Holy Spirit was first designed to fill, until it was usurped by the cyphers of mathematics. In the result, as we now know, the only certainty is uncertainty — and that most surely embraces 'God' as a function of the old certainty. Science's epiphany is discredited.

It may forever rest a moot point as to whether the logic of scientific certainty destroyed itself, or whether the seeds of uncertainty were sown by a subconscious awareness, a kind of mental sickness, of knowledge's loss of meaning. Except to make meaning meaningless, what can it mean for science to have enabled mankind to destroy itself or to induce a new Ice Age? Even on a less apocalyptic level, a life will lack much sense if it is conducted in a context removed from any tenable notion of reality. Such a context could be our very own 'bread and television' society or, if you prefer, the world of the declining Hapsburg Empire, in which Freud had his necessary origins. Such worlds are places in which people have insulated themselves, not so much from 'nature' as if that were just another object, but from interconnectedness with the environment. Conceivably, there would then be no effective context at all in which to make sense of a life. For life would be cut off from its source. But maybe this actually is the condition we all find ourselves in nowadays.

Maybe the limited sense of life in which this whole discussion is couched is itself frustrating. That remains to be seen. But it is at least possible that such frustration would not even exist if meaning rather than knowledge were at the centre of our worldview. For then life itself would be rich, loaded with significance amidst a wealth of relationships, instead of weighed down with worldly goods. And implicit in such richness would abide a tacit awareness of the sense of that of which we cannot speak. 'The meaning of the world', to repeat Wittgenstein, 'lies outside the world'.

3

TO SAY THAT it is sufficient for a life to make sense in terms of its times and its civilisation may seem harmless enough. For we are all the children of our times. Yet, in the sense I would mean by 'a life', the times themselves and those who live in them have long been out of joint. A life in our culture has made apparent sense and attained an identity when a person has gained, say, some professional distinction and achieved social recognition thereby. Or, conversely, the lonely and perhaps romantic search for one's authentic self in an alien environment has exceptionally made sense of a life (one thinks of a tortured personality like Kierkegaard or Tolstoy). Nor is the pathetic aspiration for 'honours' to be despised; they at least confer an identity. For by far the most part, however, Eliot's bleak picture of the masses in our impersonal society rings more true.

Unreal City
Under the brown fog of a winter dawn
A crowd flowed over London Bridge, so many,
I had not thought death had undone so many...
Flowed up the hill and down King William Street,
To where Saint Mary Woolnoth kept the hours
With a dead sound on the final stroke of nine.

To eradicate this stain from our culture is comparable to Lady Macbeth washing her hands of blood.

One symptom of the extraordinary transformation of the times we live in, however, is that the very distinction between a life and its world is in growing question. The mechanistic paradigm of Descartes turned the metaphysical person into nothing but a player of roles, a set of individual objects, each but an atom in the separate order of the social world, and a prey to manipulation. The new paradigm, however, is changing the very meaning of a 'life', for it relates each life indissolubly to its environment; they must become commutable, each in terms of the other.

Given that Western civilisation is premised on the separation of man from the world, this change is quite extraordinary. Descartes merely gave the separation in question its contemporary form: 'rational idealism' by name. The change now in train is from a yet more profound antecedent. Long before him, the monasteries of Christendom had already established themselves as the cradles of the industrial revolution and of the bureaucracies of the nation state.

I would indeed surmise that 'Christianity' can only be practised in the apartness of monasteries; for Christianity is merely a religion, not a way of life. 'No monkery in Islam,' said Mohammed. For Islam does not conceive of itself as a religion, but as a way of life, just as it is not concerned with knowledge in a vacuum and for its own sake. Indeed, I wonder if in the whole world there is any other 'religion' than Christianity. Are not all the others, onto which it is we who have projected the name 'religion', merely ways of living? And is this not because Christianity, through the trinity, has uniquely preserved a link between God and man, and hence claims present access to the Truth? Why else should this be, though, than because Christianity was, and immutably is, a religion of slaves, of the poor who are always with us; and ultimately, slaves of original sin? (A discovery which suddenly shocked Simone Weil.) It conquered, not by its own force, but first by becoming indispensable to its Roman masters and then turning their own force against them (cf. Romans 13). It stole their hierarchies, their systems of government, even their purple; it even institutionalised martyrdom. Christianity hinges on human weakness. The strength of the church's appeal has lain paradoxically in its other-worldliness. It has had difficulty in seeing itself as integral to the world it nevertheless aspired to dominate — except, perhaps, during the inquisition. Inherently, it needs the connivance of agents. Christians were originally told they must render unto Caesar that which is Caesar's, and to God that which is God's. Not only was this very convenient for Caesar, but it relegated Christianity proper — which, if anything, is about God — to wheresoever Caesar is not: namely in the seclusion of a monastery. How long have we been held in this thrall!

As soon, however, as we recognize that life is not really about heaven to come (just compare an Islamic burial ground, say, with the forlorn pomposity of an Italian or Victorian cemetery!), but about the empirical world, then all the priest-like authority by which we are still ruled loses its potency. That hallowed authority exuded by the experts, by the aloof professions, and the secretive mandarins of government, is nothing but a residue of the hold over us by the metaphysics of Christianity. Life, in this light, now begins to assume a mantle that could never be filled by even the sum of all technical expertise. If a life and the world in which it is lived are integral, each to the other, then sense can no more be made of that life in the world than the world makes sense of itself. Both are mysterious. But, of course, this is as much as to allow that the anthropomorphism that determines all our attitudes — the 'arrogance of humanism', in David Ehrenfeld's phrase — is deeply suspect. And this includes, let it be said, the kind of 'environmentalism' which supposes the environment exists for, and apart from, mankind.

4

IF THE END of the disassociation of person from world is now hopefully in sight, then so must be the end of romanticism: the antidote that has kept us sane. Rousseau's 'natural man' was the first expression of this. And Blake's allegory of Albion in conflict with industrialism has classically served as the shadow to rational idealism. Romanticism has always been a minority strain, but one the majority (as through the wealthy's patronage of the arts) has uneasily known it must support to keep the whole edifice of civilisation intact.

The artist and the hero (or anti-hero) have been the archetypal creatures of romanticism; both are beings somehow outside the law. Likewise the narrative (contained as it is from the world through its beginning and its ending), the concerto (that dialogue between the one and the many), or the framed figure in the landscape, these have been prime forms of the romantic movement. But now all that is ailing too. Art feeds on art with a mannerism unparalleled in history, and the gulf between 'art' and life has surely become unbridgeable. Meanwhile, as the men to whom we look for heroic leadership (JFK and that ilk) are found to have feet made of the clay of these times, our heroes too are proving even more inapposite.

All this, then, must go back into the melting pot. And with it must go 'education', itself a microcosm of both the rational-romantic balance and the conspiracy of knowledge. For Rousseau, after all, was also the inventor of 'progressive' education: an education concerned with the child as a child, an aspect of the metaphysics of the person. Out of this, indeed, grew our concepts of child psychology and the stages of childhood. This notion of progressive education, though always a minority concern, has endured as a standing challenge to orthodoxy, to Locke's notion that a child is a *tabula rasa*, passively waiting for knowledge to be inscribed upon it. Out of that orthodoxy itself there came, inexorably, education as social engineering: preparing the child like an object for some place in the world (even if sometimes to change that world). But, today, the conflict of educational persuasions has itself gone stale. The educators have all equally lost faith in themselves. The world for which they would prepare children is itself in disarray. And that disarray has stemmed from the very kind of knowledge that they would impart.

Meanwhile, the 'progressives', far from triumphing over the demoralisation of the orthodox opposition, are finding that their position is but the other side of the very same coin. (Just as the romantic movement as a whole acted as but the counter to rationalism.) Hence they are also finding that 'child-centred' education has degenerated into mere egocentricity. The significance of this is that the very force of romanticism, the ground from which it was able to challenge rationalism, initially lay in the tacit discourse about the person and the world. That the child could ever have been deemed a being in its own right (an idea that goes back before Rousseau and his 'Emile' to Christ) was because the separateness, and indeed the sacredness, of the person has always been held as a tenet of our civilisation, inherent in the dualism of its thought. But now, even that is in question.

5

THE ENDEMIC DUALISM of Western thought seems to stem from our monotheism. Because God is one, and hence awesomely alone, there is a duality about our minds that infects all our thinking. This duality, in any case, can be seen in the classical scientific detachment of observer from observed, or in our manipulation of nature (and one another) without compunction, or just in our love of idealistic abstractions like 'mankind' — in such marked contrast to the frequent meanness of our behaviour towards actual people in our lives. Because Jehovah is up there — apart, in solitude, superhuman — our dualistic cast of mind is sanctioned. For once we have posited Jehovah, both 'his' received view of the reality of the world and our view of its appearances must somehow cohabit in the repository of our minds.

Yet perhaps it is only a certain temptation, one exerted by the in-bred reverence in which we hold 'God', that leads me to this speculation? Maybe the dualism of our language itself created monotheism? Or perhaps it doesn't really matter. Nonetheless, some such chemistry must have been at work in that merging of Judaic monism and Hellenistic dualism which generated Christianity. (I know this is to set aside the all-pervasive Shamanism of those times, which the gospels so closely reflect.) Our reverence of the monotheistic idea of God has merely served to preserve our actual dualism from questioning. For at the very inner core of our dualistic minds is idealism, with all its subversive power: as Wittgenstein said, the spectacles through which we look at the world and never take off the ends of our noses.

To break the spell of the ideal is the immense task facing any change of thought that could match up to the perils of our situation. The ideal, after all, has its roots in such gaping dichotomies as those between the person and the world, the inner life and the world about us. No social edifice, for instance, can be constructed by using people as its building blocks; for a person is autonomous, and not just an amalgam of roles. Indeed it is only roles that can be used as the ultimate building blocks of any society. Significantly, only theistic societies resist this as a problem. In such societies religion incorporates the person as well as his government; medieval Christendom, of course, had this characteristic in large measure. So in a non-theocratic society, we seek to bridge these chasms in the continuum of our thought by the notion of essences. We call the very ideas of things in aid of their appearances. It is out of these reifications that we have fabricated our present world.

To do this, however, we still need God, for his providence must watch over us as we make these abstractions in order to lay claim to our share of the spoils of his universe; for there is a dualism implicit in every monism. And this necessary God must be one and uniform, if all the moral distractions, to which each of us in the course of this pursuit is subject, are logically to be composed. Moreover, he had also better be male, the father, since he is the provider with whom we have conspired to manipulate the world. This indeed is the trap into which the now desolate and godless West (for God has gone on holiday, taking our language with him, and the other gods are dead) has fallen through our fixation upon the chimera of things, and hence upon a heaven where in substance they shall be found. It's called materialism.

To escape from this trap, it is totally improbable that we could go all the way back to the beginning and revert, say, to that more inward-looking form of Christianity called Gnosticism. For this form long ago succumbed to the structured, hierarchical organisation of the trinity-based church. It is scarcely less probable

(though quite logical) that we could escape this trap
through Buddhism. Many in the Christian West are
turning in this direction, in a way that would have seemed incredible a few years ago. It would certainly have
surprised William James, whose classic *Varieties of
Religious Experience* was really about Christian religious experience alone — a fact which has seemed un-
remarkable to subsequent generations of admiring cri-
tics. Whatever our straits, however, it is barely conceivable that Buddhism's forms would prove culturally assimilable in the foreseeable future, short of the veritable
collapse of our social fabric. Zen Buddhism, it's true,
because it is pragmatically bent towards everyday life,
may have some capacity to establish itself, Samurai
fashion, in the West. But it is precisely too rigorous a
practice to consort easily with our ingrained hedonism.
That way of life must somehow be changed in its own
terms, and one can only say that logically the possibility
of this happening exists.

The possibility exists because Western thought has of
itself come to recognise that the materialistic continuum
upon which our idealistic cast of mind is founded is illusory. This is partly apparent in the discontinuities and
inherent uncertainties of quantum mechanics, as well as
in the indications from sub-particle physics that matter is
itself process (Buddhism's vindication by Western
science!). Of perhaps yet wider implication (though surely
from the same philosophical root) is the recognition that
the ultimate reality we have so long pursued — whether
of the internal or the external world — is in fact a construct of language; and yet that language is incapable of
depicting reality itself.

All this effectively destroys the idealistic framework of
our thought. And while this may seem to leave us with no
ground to stand upon, if we were courageously to re-start
our historical journey from the point to which our own
mistakes have brought us, rather then from some unimaginable clean slate, there is still the possibility to be

explored that we might discover more than we had supposed in the dormant fabric of our heritage. How much less tortured these questions about life would then become!

6

I T IS UNAVOIDABLE that we should speak of paradigms. For a life to make sense, it requires a pattern to which to conform. Indeed, cultural paradigms may well develop in response to this necessity. For the ways in which we make sense of the world, given all its bewildering variety, engender manifold analogies in our mental constructs. Thus Hobbes called upon Galileo's help in positing his Leviathan: that depiction of the central power of the state to which, he said, we must all submit. In declaring, on account of our inherent restlessness, that 'the natural state of Man is Warre', Hobbes drew, paradigmatically, on Galileo's view that all things are naturally in motion. Likewise, Jefferson penned the definitive statement of modern political democracy (the Declaration of Independence) by drawing on the Newtonian universe. For Newton's model suggested to Jefferson an orderly society of morally equal and hence atomistic individuals, whose 'natural rights' acted as the social gravity of a providential system. At all events, the paradigm that has held sway these four hundred years is (recalling Bacon's dictum) that of knowledge. And whatsoever knowledge tells us, that must be obeyed.

The 'knowledge' in question is reductionistic: what we know is achieved by analysing the whole down to its last particle. This is the regime that has produced the specialists, the experts, the professions, each in their own compartments — and each compartment a citadel of power. When Yeats said of our times, 'Things fall apart, the centre cannot hold', he was speaking of the providence that holds together this whole structure of disparate parts.

Yet there have always been shadowy alternatives to this dominant regime. There has, for instance, been knowledge by doing — a kind of knowledge given expression in our times through American pragmatism and the educational philosophy of John Dewey that grew out of it. (Such knowledge, of course, is common to those civilisations in which 'religion' is but a way of life.) There have also been utopias, which tried to put back together what our minds had taken apart, but inevitably failed to do so, just as the pieces of Humpty Dumpty could not be put back together again. (Even Francis Bacon conceived of New Atlantis, where the gravitas of science benignly ruled — but his Utopian fragment was, significantly, left unfinished.) And there have been innumerable communes, in which a regime of sharing was to have replaced that of the individual possessiveness which, increasingly, has kept the real world spinning.

The Shakers were one of the most remarkable of such communes, for, as children of the industrial revolution, they sought to combine community with technology — that technology which, of itself, tears us apart. That they lasted so long (about one hundred and fifty years) and produced so many ravishingly simple but practical artifacts was no doubt partly due to their common faith and its unaffected proletarian origins. But it was also due, alas, to their stern celibacy, for they held that once a person had found the Lord, then logically no repetition of the finder's life itself could be justified. Perhaps only some such perverse, if sterile, resolution could have accounted for the durability of a community that went against the corrupt current of the world.

And yet, people still seek community, in spite of the fact that under the regime of rationalism the very word 'community' has been sullied. For the idea of community does not lend itself to measurement; it speaks of wholes rather than parts. Yet community is, in simple terms, the only apparent way out of the trap we are in. This is so because the idea of community betokens a shift in our ruling paradigm. The deceptive certainty of that paradigm, the measurability of things, is now gone and we can no longer live at one with the world on such terms.

7

THE OLD, but still ruling paradigm was couched in terms of the measurable, of whatever could be counted. It was quantitative. The future paradigm will surely be qualitative. This follows ineluctably from the realities of language. All that language (even mathematical language) tells us is this: that it is just language; it depicts nothing — and only language can save us from language. Through language we make a world to live in that is inescapably false, and all we can do is rectify the fallacies of language by language. There is no world that is not false. What is not false is not the world. Language accompanies our lives, and its fictions are their facts. Since society, then, is construed through language, it is the meanings language conveys that matter; and meanings consist, not in language itself, but in how we use it, in its grammar. The grammar itself is only intelligible in qualitative terms. Hence, in construing language, we illuminate rather than explain the world to one another.

The practical direction in which this recognition must lead us, then, is simply towards societies of an intelligible size (as it did the Greeks): societies that can be comprehended as a whole. The thrust of quantitive knowledge, however, has led in the opposite direction: to bigness of scale. This is because reductionistic knowledge favours centralisation. Knowledge means power, and that leads to secrecy. For power, by its very nature, is something the few prefer to keep to themselves. And, moreover, the greater the area the centre controls, the greater has its validity been assumed to be, because 'truth' is quantitative.

But size has also become inchoate. It is meaningless to those — say, the inhabitants of any of our vast and sprawling cities — whose lives are dominated by it. Likewise, language of its nature can posit no certainties, no final truth, about society, or, indeed, the world. Hence the reality about language nullifies totalitarian ideology and suggests instead a kind of spiral in our affairs: an interaction between ourselves, who use language, but a relationship that never returns to quite the same place.

However, the more we separate the world into the insulated compartments associated with the languages of specialisation, the more we neutralise this dynamic interaction. Hence we 'live together' nowadays only in a weak manner of speaking. We keep the Jaguar outside the front door to make sure we are at least somebody in a sea of anonymity; for any pattern that would give meaning to our alienated and suburbanised lives has become very tenuous.

It is the case, nevertheless, that just to reduce the scale would not of itself eliminate the compartments. A small town is certainly more sociable than a large city. It means, perhaps, that people with whom you work may also be people you meet on the street, and this may warm your heart — if only by reminding you that your life has many dimensions to it. But mere smallness of scale does little more than hold out a promise of life that our culture can only the more disappoint. It may result only in parochialism. For our specialised languages remain arcane to one another; we guard our specialisations for the mystifications they afford. No wonder the English pub thrives on such common ground as there is to our lives. But even the pub, that bulwark of our civilisation, has its limitations so far as any illumination of the sense of our life is concerned. In effect, under the regime of all things quantitative, the pattern that must enrich our lives with meaning has been fragmented. Our quantitative riches are ultimately incapable of providing any sense of fulfillment. For, as all decadent civilisations have shown, one can be sated with material wealth and yet be impoverished of the wealth of meanings that life offers only in the living of them.

8

THE FORMS OF LIFE that embody a dynamic interplay between persons and an ever-changing world are almost vestigial now. Perhaps the monasteries at their height (though fatally flawed) came close to it, as did communities like the Shakers. And perhaps the great estates (which, in this respect, succeeded the monasteries) in their classical form did so as well. Although in such miniature worlds each person had his place and practised his particular skills, he also had some understanding of others' languages, because all were personally interdependent upon each another.

This is not to ignore the political context of those historical institutions, or to put a rosy hue on the paternalistic stewardship of such estates, which in terms of today's values clearly cannot be justified. That they proved politically untenable, however, does not mean they have nothing to tell us about life. For even the politics by which today we judge such bodies is itself a facet of the paradigm that supplanted them, of which the values must now in their own turn be judged. Those small worlds succumbed to the macrocosm brought into being by the high, idealistic abstractions — like the very concept 'society' — conceived, surely, in the hope of restoring coherence to the fragments into which the paradigm of quantitative knowledge has remorselessly broken down the wholeness of all traditional forms of life.

The nation state, for instance, expanded politics to the boundaries of a common tongue, but it did so at the dire cost of impoverishing each language itself. For the meanings of words have become standardised as their resonances were ever more deadened, the poetry lost, by politically imposed stereotypes. Standardised language, indeed, became a controlling instrument of the state itself. And ideology — that ultimate plague of our politics — followed upon this. For any ideology is a pretension to know political reality from that detached 'scientific' standpoint the paradigm of knowledge assumes towards the world: the ultimate devaluation of objectivity. So the validity of those ancient forms of life that once provided us with a qualitative dimension is not entirely disqualified by their having succumbed to an overweening politics, a politics fit only for gigantism. It was Martin Buber, one recalls, who taught us to use again the 'I-Thou' word to match the new forms of life we now need to forge for our own salvation, and to give renewed expression to an old meaning.

9

THE PATTERN is what gives meaning to the part. Take away some part, and, if a pattern is thereby disrupted, it must have been meaningful to that part. The world itself, therefore, can have no meaning in the world. For Wittgenstein, all ultimates within the world were 'forms of life'; that is, whenever such an ultimate was reached in language, with all explanation exhausted, then 'my spade is turned': that is, the rest was silence —

a silence that also spoke, but spoke of pragmatic uncertainty.

What forms are there, then, of life itself? They are, surely, manifold, and it is the very mentality of the current paradigm that inhibits us from seeing them under our noses. For we still proceed, in our ideas, by reducing things to their parts to see by what mechanism they work. These parts belong to no pattern, or if they do, it is soon lost and dropped off as of no importance, as an embarrassment. For the pattern can only interfere with the process of simplification by which alone we hope to understand how the part to which we have reduced our problem works. Yet these original wholes do remain, as wholes, inalienable to our everyday lives.

So, both in church and in state, we perforce devise hierarchical structures to rationalise our reductionism. These hierarchies are of higher and lower orders of structure, such that any lower order is assimilable into a higher. This assimilation is possible so long as the criteria of inclusion in one order of a hierarchy are compatible with the criteria of another. This, in turn, is as much as to speak of functions, some of which can be performed at one level, others at another, but the very performance of which is conducive to the establishment of hierarchy — whether from chapel to cathedral, or from village to city. The principles governing the priest are compatible with those of the bishop, and the village is of one family with the city.

Reductionalistically, therefore, we look to functionalism to give meaning to the forms we have: a village is what supports a church, a town a secondary school, a city a cathedral and a university. Hence, one would think that if there are any 'forms of life' itself, these presumably should be those of the highest order of some hierarchy. And yet there are none such. There is no point, no measurable size, at which a town turns into a city, or ceases to be a village. A village may have no church, a city no cathedral, and a town may have a university. Rather, these are all forms of our lives, and indispensable to discourse between ourselves. None can be subsumed in the other, nor projected upon them. They are, of themselves, qualitative, and to impose hierarchical functions upon them — as planning theory does — is an act of barbarism. There isa no order of precedence in the forms of life.

So the children of a village may go to 'school', as part of some educational hierarchy, but they will alas cease to be educated by the village. Does this not raise, then, a radical question about 'education'? The duality of child-centred and social engineering practices hereby dissolves into the perspective of the child as integral to the community, and therewith the disappearance of the gross artificiality of subject-based learning.

10

T O SAY THAT a life is part of its place and time would be unexceptional. To say, conversely, that its place and time are but parts of a life would be controversial. For this challenges our deterministic presumptions at their roots. It is not just to say that a life makes sense only as it partakes of its historical epoch, even though that would be to question whether a life is in any way unique. Rather, it would be to say that the sense of the world is implicate in the pattern of each and all our lives.

To hold this notion would satisfy our feelings for the uniqueness of any life, but it would challenge our historical presumptions. For it would say that, to make sense, a life must conform to a pattern; and that to realise this conformity it must be possible for it to discard whatsoever in its historical times might have failed to serve that imperative. This would imply that we would never allow our lives to be determined by events: to the point that events

themselves might even cease to be intelligible, cease to
have value. Implausibly, perhaps, this would make mere
accidents of space and time. Nonetheless, this is seemingly the conclusion reached by Wittgenstein, albeit by
another and firmer route, at the end of the *Tractatus*.

Any arbitrary shifts in the values of a life would indeed threaten any pattern in it. By contrast, if the world
is to be encapsulated in a life, a rigorous responsibility
surely rests upon that life to discipline itself and not
lapse into anarchy. Solipsism has its own constraints.
This is not to bespeak the monastery, with all its codes
of conduct. More likely, in practice, it is simply to talk of
some supportive community in which the exigencies of
life are not too volatile. It is certainly to speak more of a
way of life than of a faith, but it is also to recognise the
inwardness of the discipline that a life must impose
upon itself. For, in any case, the pattern of a life is
always in the making, always in process (the search is
never done with), so that no fixed rules can fashion it.

When all is said and done, however, the requisite form
of a life presumes a reciprocity between the self and the
world. It is neither of the self nor the world alone, then,
that we need to speak. And this, surely, is distinct from
the immemorial (and opposing) concerns of both East and
West: either to lose the self, or to find it. It is a concern,
rather, with what is neither the self, nor the world. It
accepts as unquestionable the tension between the consciousness of a life and the terrible immensity surround-
ing it, and it makes of this tension the unquestionable
reality — the new *cogito*, or point of origin of our philosophy.

The cost of doing this is to renounce all ultimate
explanations of what we are doing here, and all hope of
comfort from any such information. But its recompense is
the tempering of our incurable and unrequitable curiosity
by a pervasive sense of awe, which is the only sense
beyond sense itself. In other words, the poetic — which is
perhaps why for the Greeks a poet meant a maker.

To accept this cost is feasible only if the inwardness it subscribes to is of a 'knowledge' at least the peer of that which is 'out there'. In other words, a gnosticism: a knowledge communicable by poetic sympathy, by what the unspoken makes it unnecessary to say in prose, by sharing a way of life, by the processes of doing things with, instead of against, the dumb and natural world.

This gnosticism is actually nothing but 'knowledge' of our unspoken common assumptions. Yet, when that knowledge itself undergoes change, how is it then to be spoken of? When the great sea-changes, the shifts of paradigm occur, the Galileos will no doubt rise from their knees muttering their *epure se muoves* — and so things will seem to go on as before.

If changes in what is unspoken nevertheless come about, as they did despite Galileo's penitence, it is presumably because different things are seen to be done. If heaven is no longer up in the sky, it is rather because the Manchester to Bridlington railway was built, than because we all understand Newton's model of the universe. If changes in the forms of life themselves are brought about, then inward knowledge also changes. The very existence of this inward knowledge, however, alone makes bearable the cost of our never being able to know the truth overtly.

11

I F LANGUAGE does not indeed picture reality, consider the crimes that have been committed under its false prospectus! The nation state took government to the boundaries of each tongue, and did so on the premise that its commands in that tongue carried the justification of truth. The meanings conveyed by the grammar and the very accents of the governing class thus became instruments of power because they bore all the weight of knowledge, as Latin formerly had done when the church crossed the boundaries of governments. The new secular knowledge was available in the common tongue and thus to the nation which spoke it, so conferring power upon it. The 'educated classes', of course, harnessed that power, while the nation at large concurred in this centralisation. The demotic language, after all, was not merely useful; it commanded the truth. Nationalism implied truth and power, and this meant the well-being of all who spoke in a given tongue — at the cost only of other men and the languageless world.

The nation state has thus been a prime product of dualism, insofar as language, if held to depict reality, becomes the tool of dualistic thought. For the notion of 'reality' is itself a function of dualism: the atomistic, building-block notion of 'substance' being dualistically complementary to the notions of 'ideas' and the 'mind' that contains them. Language passively lends itself to this mould of thought so long as our use of it allows of 'reality' to be described. However, with the collapse of language to this claim (as it has collapsed), the legitimacy of the nation state itself is philosophically undermined. From this perspective, then, one can readily recognise that much for which central authority must take responsibility (inflation, the proliferation of nuclear arms, etc.) has its origin in dualism.

Mechanistic interpretations of such ills as these are offered in greater profusion by 'social science', all subsuming the interplay of mens' minds and the material elements, the goods, concerned. Thus monetarism assumes certain psychological responses on the 'demand' or the 'supply' side; and these assumptions further presume the inherent tendency, the 'hidden hand' of self-interest, on which Adam Smith first premised the viability of the economic system — namely, greed or utility, or whatever is the supposed nature of the reaction of men's minds to economic facts. Such is a necessary premise about the equilibrium of the purely metaphysical nature of that system.

If, however, the mechanisms in question are found not to work, it must cast doubt, not just upon the correct assessment of the stimuli in question, but on the assumedly closed nature of the system of action and reaction. Thus, if the public money available for schools, hospitals, housing, roads, etc., is reduced by central government, people may not react rationally — i.e. according to the economic model — because these things are but elements of an environment which itself is modified by their loss of provision. Moreover, because taxpayers as such are not responsible for operating such services, the money they cost has little meaning — so let inflation rip! Likewise, if taxes are reduced or increased, people may not react rationally in terms of the 'market economy', but prefer to go fishing, say, or to engage in illegal economic activity. The so-called management of the economy has become a matter of Keynesian aggregates — GNP and so forth — which supposedly are governable by official action. Such entirely metaphysical notions, however, have only made still more tenuous the implicit contract between each citizen and the value of the currency of his nation state. Far from controlling inflation, therefore, the very centralisation of government is its deepest cause.

The dualism, the kind of knowledge, inherent in the nation state abides in its structure of government and, in proportion as it puts society at the service of that knowledge, robs life of meaning. For meaning lies in pattern and in the connections of the pattern: not in knowledge. Thus it lies in the uses of language, rather than in what language ostensibly describes. Hence it lies in the reciprocity between observer and observed, in the language game, within some form of life. In other words, it lies in non-dualism.

Or consider how the nuclear arms race is driven forward because the nation state is in thrall to knowledge!

The opposing powers are armed far beyond the bounds of their own security, for every increase makes the author of that increase less secure. This is crazy — even in mechanistic terms! The mechanistic international politics of the balance of power thus runs out of control — just as do the politics of inflation and unemployment. Diplomacy is reduced to roulette. But dualistic knowledge lies at the core of the nation state; without it, that state would cease to exist. Even statesmanship and military power are subordinate to it. Its flawed understanding of life will yet take us all at once to the grave — not least, because there are none so blind to it as the intellectuals, our ruling caste. And dualistic thought is intellectually rampant.

The replacement of the nation state by the local state — wherein form would determine the functions of everyday life — is therefore of the utmost priority. In this respect, our citadels of learning are all too well named. Their kind of learning is the bacillus of the decomposition of our way of life, and the keep of the nation state.

How can anyone truly live in such a metaphysic-ridden world?

12

PACE WITTGENSTEIN, language is the cage in which we pass our lives. It separates us from the world: indeed, it generates the very difference between us and the world. Subject and object are endemic in language: the speaker and the spoken, self and non-self. Ultimately, in its own logic, language fragments the world into the atoms Democritus posited (as democracy now would atomise us) yet still leaves us the puzzle of the universal. Within language itself is all the duality of mind and matter whereby we have sought to grasp reality, but which, as only a little silence can make us realise, separates us, not so much from reality — which is itself a function of that dualism — as from whatever might be when language is not. (William Blake had virtually to invent a private language to make the point.) No wonder the Christians say, 'In the beginning was the Word,' or go on to say, 'And the Word was God'; or the Koran, that we are the 'Peoples of the Book'!

Out of this opaque awareness of some kind of separation, then, comes a perennial aspiration for wholeness, bringing with it, unfortunately, all the tyrannies of religion and ideology, all the guises of certainty, all the monistic exclusions of one part of dualism by the other. The trinity sought to make our cage orderly and habitable by embracing the duality, so that no one would realise it was a cage. Islam denied the trinity, and instead turned the cage into poetry through the Koran, but neverthless left God where he was, not so much the invention of man, as the marvel of language. The Buddhists, however, disinvented God; Zen, in particular, speaks in riddles and makes fun of language as such.

Zen, indeed, is not so much holistic as non-dualistic. Like Wittgenstein, it wants to show the fly the way out of the fly-bottle — out of the false wholes in which we take refuge. Yet even Buddhism cannot repudiate speech, and so cannot help allowing for our humanity. To be free of possessiveness, after all, is hopefully not to suspend rational speech. Or is it? Indeed, all faiths that fail to confront the paradox of language must be flawed. (And if they do confront it, will they still be faiths?) This is not implicitly to condemn us, however, to the tyranny inherent in the dualism of language. We need not accept language as a curse laid upon mankind; for we are now alerted to the dualism of mind and matter, of the grammar of subject and object, as discredited ways of making sense of life (consider only the expropriation of the world's resources to which they have led), let alone as means of freeing us from the cage of language. So this is not quite the end of the story.

In fact, the case is not one of *mind* and *matter*; rather, it is perhaps one of mind *or* matter. For language is such that when used one way, it cannot be used the other. Persons, even in their multiplicity, do not compound the world; and the whole world cannot account for any one person. Nature and nurture, in another parlance, have their separate logics. When one of these is spoken of, the other cannot be implied.

This realisation is, charitably speaking, what deeply underlay the doctrine of the trinity, of the separation of God into two parts, with the holy ghost as the medium required by logic between them, between the inwardness and the outwardness, the personal and external worlds. Yet the holy ghost is perforce posited to allow for the pitiful condition of man, who cannot endure the prospect language offers him of life, and so takes shelter from it in a language-made world. The holy ghost reconciles the Christian monotheist to the division of God, allowing him to be both subject and object, thereby restoring man's lost wholeness. To recognise, then, that when we speak of the world we can know nothing of the person, and vice versa, actually demands only one concession: the renunciation of certainty.

Language, however, is what excludes us from certainty. We have searched for certainty in the West these thousands of years, but we might as well call off the whole wasteful exercise. That waste has reached its climax with the authority presently conferred upon knowledge — a knowledge that is now seen to be meaningless. To call off the search might seem implausable, of course, if only because we seem always on the point of the next great discovery, which will resolve everything and show us the mind of God. Moreover, to call it off would possibly be to re-open the door to arbitrary political power. But we would not have to stop practising science, for example, unless, of course, science turned itself into something else:

mysticism, perhaps. Nor would we have to deny our personal integrity. We would have to accept, not just that neither of these separate logics, the logic of subject and of object, has primacy over the other, but that they are not to be reconciled by fabricating some other primacy over them both. We have, in other words, to live with the difference between them, for that is in the nature of language.

Life is a pulse of varying rhythms, constantly alternating between the person and the world. We can still make approximations; we need not be bereft of all comment upon life. Also, because we must accept the finite (or quantum) nature of what we speak about, we shall find we address ourselves increasingly to the meanings of things: that is, to how our actions fit the patterns within which life occurs. The forms life takes, because they are only approximations, remain the saving grace of the uncertainty with which language obliges us to live. And the language of forms is the language of quality, not quantity.

As for reductionist analysis, that all too powerful tool, no doubt we shall always use it as long as the parts of things to which it is applied hold meaning in terms of the wholes implicate in them. Only what is meaningless — as 'pure' knowledge is — will cease to be explored. That is the void which increasingly will be repudiated in the great sea-change of values now upon us. In terms of those values, environmental wealth — the wealth conferred by our surroundings, by the forms in which we meaningfully participate — rather than wealth measured impersonally in some metaphysical 'market', will increasingly guide our explorations. For we shall have to live with the earth, not consume it. For the cost of blind, irresponsible knowledge will be less and less affordable.

We cannot escape the dualism inherent in language; for we are condemned to speak. But in speaking of that about which we should be silent, we have fabricated a world in which we can lead only impoverished lives: a world of reifications too large and remote to be meaningful unless we shut ourselves into one or another of its compartments. The perfection we crave through language ends — unless it be in the irrational resonances of poetry — by making our lives sterile. And the greater part of this sterility is in the obstructions we make between ourselves and the world, a world we share with all else in it and that is implicate in us.

13

IMAGINE A LABORATORY of holism, a laboratory for the living practice of non-dualism! What would such a living holistic laboratory be like?

It certainly would not be anything like a community bound by some common faith. It would not be monastic in kind. Why? Because this would be 'holistic' only in the sense of being characteristically corporate, committed to the attainment of some common purpose. In so being, it would be exclusive — perhaps even antipathetic towards those who do not share its objectives (unless they were merely anodyne). It could be argued, of course, that our laboratory might be some order of mendicant monks; for such an order could scarcely be corporate in kind. On the contrary, such a model may be what the logic of non-dualistic thought, with its end of non-attachment, might point towards. But from whom would our mendicant order beg without thereby dualistically sanctioning the attachment of others?

Nor would our holistic laboratory be some kind of commune in which all goods are held in common. And why? Well, apart from the well-known and hopeless track-record of such exercises, because of the inverse of the above reasoning. Because, short of a common faith (or of a charismatic, but mortal, leader), no such sharing of goods would endure, Our experiment must at least appear to be realistic. Any worthwhile laboratory of holism has to accept technology and, therewith, all the specialisations that divide us.

Our laboratory, while not being exactly a mirror of the world, should sufficiently reflect its complexity. It should partake of the world's diversity, and its activities should include the industrial as well as the arts, the commercial as well as the educational, the agricultural and the spiritual, etc. The experiment with which it should be charged would be that of reconciling all these activities, each with its own singular criteria, within a whole that gives meaning to each part.

Initially it would be advisable for our holistic laboratory to be small in scale, small enough for each of its separate activities at least to be conscious of the other's existence. By the same token, these activities should be physically contiguous to one another, rather than widespread. It would be preferable for the laboratory to be in a rural environment, for it is the characteristic of rural values that they are held relative to some whole. Urban values, on the other hand, are held reductionistically: what the village thinks of what you do, for instance, is a matter of indifference to a city. So we might say that our holistic laboratory should take the form of a landed estate.

Even assuming that we have such a setting, by what conceivable means could the inherently diverse activities in our laboratory make sense as part of the pattern of a whole?

Initially some kind of common ownership, some entrustment of all the assets of the laboratory, might do the trick. But, in fact, this would not suffice: it may be a necessary, but not a sufficient, condition. For the different criteria of these diverse activities could, by themselves, allow of no agreement as to how resources should be used. Disagreements over this would tear the laboratory apart. At the very least, they would place great strains upon even the most benign control of its activities.

In simple terms, one will find oneself searching for a common humanity in all this diversity. (Even this is too simple. Our search should not be confined just to the human relationships in the laboratory. Yet maybe this offers a clue.) What is common to humanity is language. But it is precisely language which divides specialisations from one another. Yet it is only divisive because of the widespread illusion that language *describes* the reality of the world. Through our supposed realism, we actually lose contact with one another, and thus destroy the patterns that might lend meanings to our lives. In other words, specialists have no right to appropriate to themselves, or monopolise, the meanings of a language. Therefore, our attention should be fixed on the inalienable ambiguity of language.

This suggests that in our holistic laboratory those engaged through industry or commerce in the creation of wealth, should realise that there are more meanings to 'wealth' than can be measured by money. And those whose traffic is in the arts should recognise that the professional artist does not have a monopoly over aesthetic taste. Likewise, the farmer should see that land has meanings for people other than as a resource for agricultural technology. And those whose practise is education should learn that it is not only, or even primarily, in schools that education takes place. All of this would be against the wisdom of our times; but it is only to say that, in our holistic laboratory, the environment, the climate of events, would receive priority over instrumental action.

If it is the ambiguity of language, rather than the mirage of its precision, that should be the necessary concern of our holistic laboratory, then ultimately, it is not what its members all know that will unite them, but what they all realise they are ignorant of. To bring home to people of different disciplines who are working together that the language of their particular skill is inadequate to describe the reality of what they do may seem demoralising. But it could also prove to be the beginning of spiritual wisdom. It could make us realise how unsound is the basis upon which we have built our fanatases and ideals. In getting back to the rough ground of everyday life, of living together, will we not become more aware of the mystery that surrounds us all?

Now there is, in fact, just such a holistic laboratory, It has existed since 1925 as the Dartington Hall estate in Devon. It is a trust which owns businesses with multi-million pound turnovers, that over the years has run agricultural, artistic and educational projects with national and international reputations, and that subscribes to no common dogma. Its various parts have from time to time suffered all the vagaries the world is heir to, in addition to having been subject to all the centrifugal forces of their particular kinds. Yet some mystique still holds them all tenuously together: some primordial promise of wholeness, a force of attraction to all and sundry that flies in the face of all the contemporary forces of disillusionment and disintegration, whereby to fill the spiritual vacuum those forces have created.

Dartington is beautiful and rich, and has engendered its share of illusions; but those entrusted with its destinies at least know that there is still a needle's eye to be threaded.

14

WHEN IN AMAZEMENT we ruminate (as I take it, some of us do) that anything exists at all — whether it be a speck of dust, or all the galaxies in our universe — or (as perhaps fewer of us profitably do) that were nothing to exist it would be even more amazing, then we commonly call upon the help of God. At least this is true in the West. Of course it may not be so in the Buddhist East, where religion is nominally without God, but perhaps where the question itself has been more often asked. Both in West and East the fundamental religious question is nevertheless asked. And in each case the question stems from the same root: the mortal self. Should it find itself in God, or lose itself in not-God?

Whichever of these options is chosen, it would seem to have consequences that permeate our everyday lives. And likewise, so would the variations within each option, such as, for instance, the supposed Protestant ethic of 'salvation by works.' So one does not discuss these questions for theological reasons, but rather because they illuminate our ordinary lives. To harbour personal ambition, to subject others to our power, to acquire knowledge so that we might have secrets others do not enjoy, or to pursue wealth as a yard-stick of our own importance: these are driving forces of a society in which the discovery of the self is paramount. Such is a society with its origins in belief in a personal God — that is, in God as a person (a father) — and in his providence. For this is a natural consequence of language — at least of language as something taken for granted rather than something miraculous.

We take language to picture the world, to reflect reality. So it is not, as is sometimes said, that we have invented God. God is endemic in our use of language. He has become the 'reality of reality,' the 'word' itself. It was with language that the 'peoples of the book' began. That is what made possible Jehovah's detachment from the world. Just as language separates us from the world it describes, so also is God separated from what only his language can explain. And thus he has taken on the attributes of personality, of that aloneness of the self from whence we perceive this world we but transiently inhabit.

Images of images! Are we but mirrors of mirrors? And if so, of what is 'reality' the reflection? Is there, on the one hand, the hidden order of the world, which is the inscrutable purpose of God? And is there, on the other hand, ourselves, who are in the world but not of it, the images of God, his gardeners and stewards on earth, cultivating his property as best we can? For if man is set apart from the world by language, his understanding of reality can come only from someone in whose image he is made, someone who himself made the world. As Wittgenstein said: 'If lions could talk, we couldn't understand them.' And what if God were a lion?

Yet let us suppose that language is not a reflection of the world's reality. What would then happen to this whole edifice? What then would I be? What would be the self? And for sure, language does not reflect reality; it only plays games with it. This shatteringly simple repudiation of the premise of hundreds, even thousands of years of our civilisation scarcely needs any more labouring. Language, we have come to realise, has other business than reference — even reference to the 'simples' of the atomists. It is, at the lowest, a convenience of communication. At the highest, in poetry, or in divine nonsense, like koans, it is an enchantment — to the loss of which the unpoetic, mechanical nature of our lives today bears witness. But all the richness of the subject/object grammar of our thoughts does not imply that language refers to the real: neither as object or subject.

The very richness of the English vocabulary has led us down the primrose path of reification: of finding things where no things are. In other words, I am a convenience of language. So I am not separate from the world, even though I may die and the world may be eternal. Yet nor am I not. No more, then, is God not — though 'God' also as a convenience of language cannot be. For our language makes us proud. We think we can penetrate these mysteries by our fictions; we can even assume that there are no mysteries. On this pride we build great spiritual and material edifices. Ultimately these edifices serve to defy mortality, so that whoever is most famous will 'live' the longest. Yet in relation to eternity, such edifices are not in the slightest bit different from the rest of life's transience. And sadly, this defiance of death is at the cost of much present inequity.

It is in just this inequity that egoism flourishes. Egoism divides the world up, the better to master it. Thus the discovery of the self becomes the mastery of the world. The self and the world become separate and opposite objects, identified by language and bound up with our idea of knowledge, which itself depends upon this very separation. In Christendom, the very notion of inward knowledge was banished at Nicea, in AD 323, when the Church prepared to take over the authority of Rome, and the gnostics, with their inward knowledge, were suppressed. Yet to learn by action, in contrast to reflective knowledge (theory), is to know inwardly. And if I, the doer, truly have such inward knowledge, then there must be another dimension to myself: a dimension of the spirit — or whatever it may be that stands outside the subject/object structure of our language. Likewise, inward knowledge concerns the whole of what is known, not just a part. There is no other way of perceiving the whole than inwardly; it is only inwardly that the form of which anything is a part can be known. We intuit what is whole. The I which perceives the whole does so because it is not separate from what it perceives. And that which it perceives is not separate from what it does not perceive. Thus in perceiving the part, I perceive the whole.

This inward knowledge is not the same as, nor to be confused with, what God — understood as the real self — supposedly confers. Rather, these are rivals. The latter derives from authority, from that to which language gives the status of objective reality — as the Church does to God (a status which in turn has been transferred to the State). The former derives from what seems to work in the everyday concourse of the world, from what each of us knows in his heart, or his guts, to be the case. This, rather than the

Church, is what is truly spiritual, just as doing any work
as it should be done is spiritual. For the spiritual and the
material are not separate.

But this will hardly be satisfactory for those who want
authority — whether of kings, or popes, or science. It
offers no final solution, no utopia. And, moreover, it is
largely conceived in negatives. Indeed, let us contrast the
idealistic wholeness offered by Christianity with the non-
dualistic wholeness of Zen. Which is the more honest?
Christian wholeness exists in the convolutions of the
trinity: to make one of what is incorrigibly two (the world
and the self), a third is conjured up as their solvent. This
old allegory is certainly richer than the impoverished Car-
tesian dualism of our times, where the self is a substance
'whose only purpose is to think,' but still the trinity
depends upon the literal truth of its parts: God, Christ,
church. With Zen, on the other hand, the deception of
language is understood and even joked about, such that
its (Zen's) perceptions are often couched negatively or
paradoxically. As for the rest: well, 'what we cannot speak
about we must pass over in silence.' Wittgenstein's aphor-
ism certainly has more to do with Zen than with the
context in which it was actually written.

Nowadays, we can call another analogy to our aid: that
of anti-matter. Just as space is filled with anti-matter, so
do the negatives and paradoxes of Zen have more truth in
them than all our empty positivistic rhetoric. When all is
said and done, this rhetoric stems from nothing but our
supposed mastery of the world, our limitless capacity to
know it by measuring the parts into which we have
divided it — only to find, as we now are discovering, that
nature always wins in the end, and that our very civilisation is being undermined by the alienations we have
introduced into it by our manipulation of men as objects.
Now we know that this cannot be done: that the observer
cannot he separated from the observed, that there is an
indeterminacy about the world which renders all
measurement unreliable.

We have yet to learn this, of course, insofar as human relationships are concerned, and until we do so our ideological tyrannies will no doubt continue. But events, if nothing else, will teach us that if there is to be a social science at all, far from its being 'value-free,' values must be its ever-changing yardstick. Yet as the 'I' that is so much part of the dialogue about the world eventually drops out, then the I that was excluded from the dialogue can come to know what is being talked about. But it will know it from that still place outside language — there, where it is known not only that objects are empty, but that ultimately there is neither process nor non-process in the world.

In practice, however, since language encages us with its irremediably different logics, the best we can probably achieve is an oscillation between the person and the world, an oscillation that gives each their say. Let there be no pretence, then, that there can be an ideal world subsuming the person, nor that solipsism and its anarchical world can seriously be attempted. A balanced relationship between person and world has perhaps only one fundamental requirement in our day and age: that the institutions of its discourse be small enough for the person to count as a person, such that relationships are concrete, not abstract. And that Leviathan, which through their common tongues has made but objects of people, should be dismantled. Only when that happens, shall we really use language again, which now uses us. And then we might talk of wisdom.

15

TO ASSUME GOD is not to believe in God. Of such is the decadence of our secular society: for we hold to the reifications that stem from the assumption of God, while no longer believing in God. To achieve this result, however, it is only necessary to cling to a tenet: that the fragmented world we have contrived is providentially real, and hence, as by some hidden hand, will cohere. And this is why the gathering ecological crisis is ultimately a threat to our assumptions about reality itself. It is no wonder that we are pervaded by foreboding. And it is hardly surprising that any profound questioning of the Christianity in which we no longer believe is still as profoundly resented.

Yet to call God to our aid once again is less than constructive. For language itself hypothesizes God. 'In the beginning was the Word, and the Word was with God, and the Word was God.' But the Word is potentially both subject and object, the knower as well as the known. So it was that St John promptly directed the course of official Christianity through the mystique of the Word: 'The Word became flesh, and dwelt among us, full of grace and truth; we have beheld His glory, glory as of the only Son from the Father.' By this personification the language of God was to be made intelligible to mankind, and the language of man acquired the authority of truth.

What language described could thus be nothing but real. And so we have conceived a reified world, a world of things causally driven by millenarian forces towards salvation by God, from whom we are separated only by the transparency of human grammar. The self has likewise been reified — such that the fore-doomed search for it has continued through the Christian ages; for, as knowers of the known, if our knowing is not of reality, how can we who know not be real? Yet there are civilisations, perhaps wiser than ours, whose philosophies recognise that no ontology, no notion of reality, can rest upon God; for God is a predicate of language itself, in which the word 'why', and hence the verb 'to be', is embedded. The rest of us, alas! theologise.

In the West, in particular, with our hybrid heritage of monotheism (Jewish) and idealism (Greek), the odds were stacked against the gnostic strain present in early Christianity, which offered neither certainity nor permanence. The imperatives of Roman politics prevailed over this. Whatever was said or written could thenceforth be taken to portray only the immutable, the 'objective', something concrete and absolute. For, otherwise, the reality of both the speaker and what was spoken of would be brought into question: and that would be to bring God into question. Yet in the East (not having Rome to contend with) they saw beyond all this reification. So, two thousand years ago, civilisation forked between theism and non-theism. And even if in the West today the priests of its churches may not politically count for much, they have but been replaced by their materialistic heirs: the scientists, doctors, economists — priests of that reification to which theism ineluctably resorts.

This is all the more so in the case of Christianity because of its trinitarianism. The doctrine of the trinity made the essential incomprehensibility of 'creation' tractable to hierarchical authority, in a way that all the persuasions of charismatic prophesy could never have done. But it did so at the cost of dividing man himself: of dualism, opposing mind to body, soul to matter, person to world, self to society. It was the greatest seduction in all history. Some now call for holism to bring this dualism to an end, because of the threat dualism is seen to pose to our survival in this world we have violated. Perhaps holism would be preferable to dualism, perhaps not. Holism still presupposes a subject-object relationship of language; for the whole is still an object, and so, logically, theistic. And holism could predicate a theistic society — as does Islam, for instance. Or, in its degenerate secular form, it could bespeak Marxism, or Fascism.

For holism is not the same as non-dualism, which is the mode of thought whereby Buddhism would avoid our bewitchment by language. Yet, for the Western mentality, the implications of non-dualism seem bleakly negative;

the only prescriptions it seems to offer are negative ones — of what should not be done — whilst the 'emptiness' of all concepts is the only reality. The glory of the world for the non-theist lies not in what is true, but in what is not false; it lies simply in what is — in health, rather than in heaven.

This recalls Wittgenstein's dictum: 'philosophy leaves things as they are'. Wittgenstein (whose philosophy uncannily but unconsciously echoes Mahayana Buddhist thought of two thousand years ago) being himself very much of the West, was fully conscious of how much this was asking us to accept. The best he could suggest was that the Western craving for absolutes, for making things real, should merely be indulged in order that wisdom might grow from the resultant disillusion. Yet is it not just here that the significance of the ecological is to be found? For the ecological refers to interconnectedness. It thus sees wisdom in the everydayness of life, in what transpires from moment to moment. For it is by this, rather than by any universal law, that the multifarious universe is so miraculously compounded. And to be aware of this concordance cannot be otherwise than to treat of the world as holy.

This being so, it must be our prime concern not to damage the world by abusing our faculty of language to promote the illusions of materialism. Yet to think of the world as holy in no way requires the assistance of God. Whether, however, God should be called upon for other reasons is a different question: one to do with human frailty in face of a landscape too bleak to be borne by our speech-bewitched species in its search for paradise. It is the question of whether it is practicable to suppose that civilisation can be sustained without the trappings of some system of belief in all its materiality.

This was essentially the theme of Dostoyevsky's great parable of the Grand Inquisitor (who, in compassion, had Christ burnt at the stake when he returned to earth and started disturbing the people so much). It is also raised by the question of whether Buddhism, which is not without its own concessions to human frailty, could have survived in Japan without the co-existence of animistic Shintoism, or even of today's sub-culture of the 'water trade', just as it is raised by what is to happen in the desolations of Liverpool, or Brixton. And it suggests why the materialistic West still resists any alternative to the Christianity it has essentially abandoned.

Whether mankind is inherently so frail or not, whether or not the ceremonies should be observed, what matters is that at least we should recognise our frailty for what it is. But we should not mistake our frailty — our acquisitive materialism — for strength, as now we do in rejoicing in our dominion over the earth. Our 'work', it logically follows, should become our play: at best a game, in which we confess that we need to indulge ourselves. What marvels, all around us and under our very noses, might we not then come to recognise!

16

'OUR FATHER, which art in Heaven...' which is as much, or as little, as to prescribe for each of us our separate identities. For what need is there of a father and a heaven, but to be responsible for our souls? By this compound of Judaeo-Greek ideas — of God and our ideal abode — we are condemned to seek for the self that is unattainable on Earth. The demands made through this medium are of an ultimate modesty, but the presumption of making them is unexampled.

Yet what an impoverishment of our natures is this pursuit of our supposedly real selves! For are we not, each of us, a multiplicity of persons, both at any moment and at different times? And if so, how are we separate from each other? Or even persons at all? Hence, if there is a father in a heaven who exists to discriminate between us, how shall we ever be united — as, for instance, we might be by 'love'? Only, presumably, by heaven's prescription: by prescription of our practices, our rules, laws, proprieties. And these prescriptions will no doubt be condoned by the overt differences, as of the sexes, observable between any one body and another, or generalities of bodies, observable between different societies, no matter that these differences themselves are never the same.

In other words, the language of convenient forms supports the whole realm of heaven. But worse, the worldly authority which must reign if these prescriptions are to be followed will always seek to confirm itself by establishing differences where no differences exist. And to structure our lives around 'differences' in order to preserve our separateness will be to create conventions that lack all other sanction. The categories of 'male' and 'female' come most obviously to mind, with all the taboos they entail. (And what a curious phenomenon is clothing! A language expressedly to conceal the truth.) But because of these categories, we in the West may not touch one another, and so have immeasurably diminished our emotional wealth.

Is the contemporary tendency towards 'unisex' a reaction against this obscurantism, and thus against the imposition by language of our separateness? From the same origin comes the idea of sex as something material, an object that one 'has', like fast food. The separation of lover from beloved — particularly between those of the same sex — and hence the making of 'love' as some reified ideal, as in Platonic love, has made this materiality all but inevitable. For it is the antinomian fate of all our idealisations to descend in practice to the grossest materiality. Perhaps Plato's beautiful absurdity in the Phaedrus, about the charioteer with his contrary selves in tandem, was deserving of no better outcome; for who is this real self, in charge of his better and worse selves, that he so seductively posits?

But the Greeks themselves, before they let the written word of such as Plato bewitch them — and Socrates himself had warned against the permanence of written meanings — lived in small communities, and in such communities the moderation they taught, like the Buddhists' middle way, was possible. For the middle way is nothing but recognition of the impermanence of things. What a person is today he will not be tomorrow, and even today he is not one person. Hence in small communities there is less need for depersonalisation, less need to neutralise the unpredictability of anyone's behaviour, by abstractiing 'people' from 'society'. Christianity, however, made a desperate religion for the rootless individuals of an urban society, Rome, who were at a loss where to turn, their native gods disgraced. And we have been condemned to live in that petrified forest ever since, lost in a bewitchment of authoritarian prescripts.

Perhaps the trouble with prayer is its need to use words. These tend only to make bad philosophers of us.

17

HOW DO I KNOW what pain you are suffering? I can not; it is yours. I can imagine it but I can never feel it. So, that it is pain you suffer — or that you are suffering at all — is an artifact of language. We share only a language of pain. Thus I am not sorry for you because you are in pain: rather, because I am sorry for you, I infer that you are in pain. So is it also with 'inner' knowledge. External knowledge is something you and I can verify with our senses 'objectively'. We are able to predicate that effect follows cause. But because such 'knowledge' is not actually independent of the observer — and does this compound of the senses actually exist? — it is in a real sense less truthful than the knowledge we have just from the language we share. This is a knowledge that 'leaves every thing as it is'.

However, the understanding I may have of someone else's inner knowledge will be affected by the circumstances of each case, and not least by any affection, disrespect, or fear in which I hold the bearer of it. It may be, for instance, (or might have been) of the Divine Right of Kings: of the right a king knows he has to rule over me. Or it may be of what I myself have learnt over the years of how best to farm a particular field. Or it may simply be of what you know about whom to trust, or distrust, in life. There is no certainty about all such knowledge, but it is nonetheless knowledge. It is not to be discredited just because it cannot be verified. What matters, then, is the grammar of what is private — your pain, etc.: the circumstances, that is, and how they are described, in which the use of some word has meaning, although it describes no reality that can be verified.

And this also applies to the language of specialists, which, incomprehensible to laymen, has produced the familiar 'Us and Them' syndrome of our times. Atomic physics, for example, is a subject laymen have laboriously sought to comprehend throughout recent public inquiries into atomic power, but it remains a secret to all but a few. Yet such secrets each have their grammar, which belongs to common parlance. The raw materials and the waste, the social structures involved, the costs, the location and appearance: these all belong in the domain of public expression.

The full grammar of private knowledge, in other words, is what we have come to call the 'environment.' The very notion of the environment is validated by the fact of language: that something cannot be named in isolation from the world around it. And clearly the notion of community is also validated in this way, as something to be given weight, though this cannot be measured. Conversely, the notion of egalitarianism is hereby made suspect; for what is egalitarianism but the counting of one head at a time, regardless of its context? And what is the justification of democracy, after all, except that it is arguably the least objectionable way of conducting a nation state? And what indeed is the justification of the nation state?

If the true province of knowledge is environment and community, and if reductionism is profoundly ill-conceived, then the reconsideration of Western values might be endless. Such reconsideration cannot stop short of Christianity, nor of the self which lies at its core. For this self, and concern for its salvation from original sin, is set apart: a thing knowable only to God. As such, the self projects onto the world its idealisations, always seeking to change the world, rather than taking it as it is. And we, as a civilisation, live by those artificial constructs, those reifications, and cherish them suicidally, although we have lost all understanding of the religion that brought them about.

Whatever fills this vacuum, this hollowness in how we live (as surely it will be filled) must start from the world as it is, and from this moment.

18

A ND YOU ,' asked my friend, 'what are your ideas about death? What is your formulation?' (He was, of course, French!)

'No more than I have about life,' I said, or something to that effect, 'You can't have one without the other'.

'And the soul? Is that not something apart?'.

'An invention of Plato,' I said (probably quite wrongly), 'It's all of a piece with the deceptions of idealism by which our civilisation has been bewitched, and for which it faces ruin. Along with the absurd notion of the person, and of personal existence.'

'And the spirit...?' he ventured.

Ah! the spirit. That which animates, that which over-rides the machinery of determinism, that which inheres in life, from gnats to human-kind, and perhaps even in the particles of solid matter.

Then is the spirit that which individuates the very life in which each living thing participates? In the Great Spirit, as it were (to use animistic terms)? For cannot I speak of her spirit, as of someone who is gone, but still lives? Yes, presumably I may, if I need to use the gram-mar of animism, and find my excuse for doing so in its poetry. Yet the grammar of spirit surely lies elsewhere; for if I speak of 'her spirit', then why not 'her soul?' Because, unlike soul, spirit is not attached to any person! On the contrary, the very force of spirit is as the agent of non-individuality, of the nullifier of separate, atomistic things. Spirit, then, gives life to matter and, in so doing, dissolves it.

Yet for this to happen, there must be matter to be dis-solved. There is nothing animate without the inanimate. Thus, while we live we are but enspirited, ever-changing matter. And when we die — and before we are born — we are the same. For, 'we' — you and I — are interdependent: an interdependence that underlies all the grammar of spirit. This interdependence precedes and succeeds us, whether we are born and die in a hovel or a palace. Inter-dependence thus lies in our faculty of language. Although stones and stars and other creatures may not speak, they are still spoken about. By speaking of them, they are changed and thus enspirited.

We do not see the stars now as we did before the current theories of the origins of this universe, nor as they were seen before Copernicus, or before Ptolemy, or when they were the gods themselves. For all things are the 'things' we say they are (and not other 'things!'), because the structures of our communication make them so. They are not 'really' anything at all. And a thing is not nothing simply because it is not another thing. Animation lies in language, in what it is meaningful to talk about.

So death is not a medical or a mechanical condition (for the Tibetans it does not truly occur until three days after a body has drawn its last breath). Death occurs, if at all, only when it is no longer meaningful to speak of the person or being concerned, when there is no longer any context for such discourse. Then the spirit of that person's name, at least, will be gone. But though a human being — or any creature — is so much less permanent than the stars, yet not only is it much less impermanent than its own body, but the stars themselves are a context shared and hence binding upon the spirits of all who ever gazed upon them, or ever shall. The stars enspirit us because they have been the companions of all our lives. Hence, while all things change, spirit remains so long as history lasts. Perhaps this is why All Hallow E'en was once more central to the calendar. And perhaps it means we die only when it no longer makes sense to speak of death. One might say it is only death that keeps us alive.

If spirit is not specific to a person, it does not legitimate each of our separate existences. To pursue such legitimacy is, alas, a folly. We all partake of a mystery, but separately we have no meaning and so are not immortal. The sadness of death is in its discommunication. Its chill down our spine lies in its intimation, not so much that we will cease to exist, but that the loss of communication is a matter of indifference to our very notions of existence and non-existence. 'Le silence eternel de ces espaces infinies m'effrait,' said Pascal. But I'm sure it comforted him to communicate it.

19

W HAT IS a spiritual life? One of prayer, or passive meditation? Hardly! If only because that is no 'life' at all. Then one of action and contemplation? But would that be active contemplation or contemplative action? The difference matters: for the former could be typified (at the extreme) by military church services before and after battle, whereas the latter might preclude any battle at all. Yet one must beware of caricatures; and it is all too much a sign of these times that a life of church-going on Sundays and of serving Mammon the rest of the week now comes within the bounds of caricature. That kind of alternation between our inner and outer worlds is no longer credible as a spiritual path, if ever it was.

Yet the rhythm itself still has significance. For the question remains: can matter simultaneously be spiritual, and vice versa? Or is an alternation between the spiritual and the material in one's life the more realistic scenario? Consider a farmer, for instance, whose work is his meditation. His crops, surely, would do no violence to nature, for he would not consider them alone but also his relation to them, and hence the world of which both he and they formed a part. The same would be true for his stock. Such a farmer would see things whole. And to see things whole is to live spiritually, for of the whole there is no explanation, no ultimate cause: there is only the moving spirit.

Yet would such a farmer ever see the whole whole? That is, would he not consider things sequentially, contemplating one course of action at a time? But if he fails to contemplate the overall pattern he must follow, and himself in relation to it, there can be no spirit; everything would be fixed. Indeed, for some, to follow some such a pattern would imply some ultimate cause — and they would call it

'God' no doubt, like the Amish and Mennonites do, with respect. Or is the whole accessible in one blinding, intuitive flash — as some followers of Zen would contend of enlightenment? And after that flash? While life still has to be lived, how can it be other than in the living of it that the wholeness, which is its spiritual character, resides?

Then, in the particular moments of any life, the whole, as a whole, can only remain hidden from the actor. Light does not light light. ('Light seeking light doth light of light deny.') So is a spiritual life also a chimera? Maybe so! But only if the same is true of life itself, unless, of course, there is nothing to talk about because, in a world of dead things, language has become meaningless. Hence rituals — if one cannot accept the alternative hypothesis of instantaneous revelation and subsequent perpetual ecstasy — are important for a spiritual life. They make the rhythm, the pulse, and are the tokens of wholeness. It is only when the tokens, the symbols and the language, are mistaken for the reality that degeneration occurs.

It follows, surely, that rituals should be minimal if they are not to lead us into temptation — either the temptation of supposing that spiritual life is enshrined in church or temple, or that of assuming that it has to do with the preservation of one's immortal soul. For, on the latter score, our farmer whose work is his meditation could never meditate in solitude. For his meditation must embrace others in its grammar, even if those others are only the community of his work. And he too will have his symbolism — even if it be something as generic as 'the land'. Meditation that bridges inner and outer, subject and, object, is not a practice for solitaries. It is a matter of community: for a spiritual life to be even possible, the environment must make it possible. Yet equally, without the parts — moment by moment, and piece by piece — there is no whole. A spiritual life, then, is one committed to the possibility that these parts might make a whole.

20

F ULLNESS IS NOT WHOLENESS. A full life is not a whole
life. One may taste of everything set upon the table of
life, and yet not be whole; just as one may be whole, yet
taste but little. An urban life, with all its extraordinary
variety, may be very full — albeit full in proportion to its
anomie — but there will probably be little wholeness to it,
little connection between one thrill and the next, any
more than there is between neighbours.

But a rural life, perhaps just because its opportunities
are few and technology fragments its activities less, may
(as with a craft) be a more interconnected network, and
hence be constituted of wholes larger than any in urban
life. Your stockman, for instance, will connect winter with
summer and harvest with sowing, the herbage best for
sheep with that for cattle, and will identify himself in all
manner of ways with the land and his neighbours.

There will be a wholeness about his life, such as could
not be said of your urban factory or office worker, each of
whom will desolately sense the meaninglessness of his
many but disparate activities; for he will be at a loss to
connect them. He will, of course, seek compensations —
the void in his life being such that only consolations can
pretend to fill it. So the town feeds upon the town: it is
involved in the business of sensations and can never have
enough of them. Trade is perforce self-justifying.

The emptiness proper to a spiritual life, conversely,
cannot be filled and need not be filled, for it is reality
itself. Whatever is whole is also empty, for it is its own
justification and not a product of mechanics. It is empty of
value because it is not relative. Yet it can be pursued only
in community. That the life of a hermit is ipso facto a
spiritual life is one of the West's illusions, one presumably
stemming from the idea of a soul. But such a life cannot be

private, because it cannot be lived without language, and language can never be private. Community on a human scale is thus a prerequisite of wholeness in life.

Yet the community that offers wholeness, paradoxically, is not one that altogether lacks fullness. For there can be no whole if there are no parts to be connected in it. And life will be the richer the more parts can be assimilated into any livable complex. But, one suspects, the limits of mankind's spiritual capacity are all too soon reached before he becomes surfeited with its riches.

For this reason, the proving ground of any spiritual life the future may hold is more likely to be found in the relatively uncomplicated countryside, rather than the town. And, indeed, in a countryside largely surplus to the needs of food production, and with an urban population largely surplus to employment, the destiny of the land may soon be nothing less than to test the validity of a spiritual, rather than a nihilistic, environment.

21

THE ENVIRONMENT is not determinate. In this it differs from each and every particular thing. Nor is it a thing in itself, for a thing is a thing only by virtue of its not being another thing. Not being determinate, the environment is infused with uncertainty. Those who claim to defend it, and so control it, should therefore be very careful of their credentials. Sadly, most crusaders for 'the environment' are patently motivated by one kind of self-interest or another: by their desire to possess or appropriate some part of it. But the environment is an undifferentiated whole, a process of interdependence: always, and instantly, in flux.

All this is curiously reminiscent of how St John described the quickening spirit, which like the wind 'bloweth where it listeth, and thou hearest the sound thereof, but canst not tell whence it cometh, or whither it goeth.' There is this same mysterious quality about the environment. It is, after all, the very progenitor of time; for, unlike the track of any differentiable and inherently repeatable thing, its course is irreversible, and is such as will 'wear this world out to the ending doom.' Nor can any man separate himself from this process. We each partake of it and, in so doing, sacrifice our separate identities. Nothing is outside of it, for it is not some thing that any other thing can be outside of.

All told, in fact, the contemporary concern for the environment is tantamount to a Western form of Buddhism: Buddhism without the name — and all the more Buddhistic for that. But this is also to suggest how the West has a vital contribution to make to Buddhism itself, which (whether it knows it, or not) is also in crisis. For Buddhism, starting from the premise of suffering (that is, of our illusions), may be termed the pursuit of reality through the dissolution both of concepts and of he who conceives of them: a dispersal of illusions that ends in 'form is emptiness, and emptiness is form.' Yet it is not in our flawed Western understanding of it alone that it has been construed as quietism, nihilism, or mere passivity. The East, too, has dug this trap for itself and, as a result, has become vulnerable to Western materialism.

For commonplace Buddhism has not always heeded its greatest teachers, such as Nagarjuna and Dogen, who have taught that although language (concepts) stands between ourselves and reality, words still belong in the world even though they may not picture it. (Perhaps such teachings are just too disturbing to live with.) Hence abstractions have all too commonly been used to discredit the abstract, concepts used to veil the concepts that veil reality, and meanings — as of 'being' and 'becoming,' or the 'really real' — deviously contrived to mean something else. So to counter the lures against this self-centredness, which historically was seen as the all too human lure of Hinduism, and currently is evident in consumerism, there was and is the phenomenon of Samurai Zen, where all is of the now, immediate and apparently self-less (i.e. actually corporate).

This, surely, is at the core of Japan's crisis of cultural identity, her schizophrenia in face of western materialism. In that land, of all places, the centre surely cannot hold — and assuredly not by means of the paradisaical Buddhistic populism now widely peddled there, which is as fraudulent, not just as Christian fundamentalism, but also as much of our 'environmentalism'. For Samurai Zen is not deep Zen: not the Zen that would give words their due. For even though words do not portray the world, they do allow us our humanity. In particular, while it motivates the pursuit of specific objectives, shallow, 'not-thinking' Zen, with all its one-to-one relationships, allows of pollution of the environment with impunity (vide Tokyo).

Ironically, it is the West, struggling to escape from the concepts and their sterilities by which it has been held captive, that perhaps holds the contemporary key to the preservation of the deepest values of the East. The comfort the West has to offer is not some still more convoluted use of words to describe what words ultimately cannot describe, but the notion of the language-game: that, between the ever-uncertain world and the never constant meanings of our language, there is a ceaseless interplay such that 'the meaning of a word is its use in the language'. Yet this is equivalent to saying that language itself derives its authority (for its use is not arbitrary) from the environment. Such authority comes from no particular part of the environment, such as the incorrigible temptation of humans to give names to things would suggest, but from the whole — and from the parts only insofar as the whole is implicate in them.

This authority itself is conferred, not so much by the whole of 'creation', as by those manifold wholes that occupy the logic of our daily lives, the forms of life we reach whenever our explanations grind to a halt. One would especially include among these wholes those now vestigial communities like working villages, which have been displanted in the tragedy of our culture by 'communities' of specialists and professionals, each disconnected from the other. Logically, all wholes are limited: no dialectic is otherwise possible. The Japanese, however, seem tragically to have perverted the Buddhist notion of the interdependence of all things to make a hermetic whole of Japan itself.

It follows from all this that 'reality' (as, so to speak, the 'guarantor' of language) is precisely a question that language itself is not at liberty to discuss. It does so only at the cost of trapping us in its fly-bottle. (Remember: 'The Tao that can be spoken of is not the Tao that is.') Yet reality will not be banished from our system, or our language, by edict. We must name even what we cannot discuss, because even by that denial it conceptually exists. Reality, thus understood, is the same as the spirit. It is present everywhere. And only in this sense is it 'emptiness', which is tantamount to 'fullness'.

More cogently to contemporary minds, we configure it as the 'environment'. It is in the environment that we embody the elusive quality of the real in these times of disillusion with materiality; and, for the time being, so may it serve. The environment is the surrogate, the lieutenant (lieu-tenens), of reality. But let us not deceive ourselves that therefore it is the truth itself. What it does, perhaps, is to encourage us to give primacy wherever possible to a whole over its parts. This is the enduring lesson of the environment: a lesson, ultimately, in wonder. Yet how little time we now leave, in what little time we've got left, to marvel at it all! And it is perhaps here, in the recognition that time may come to an end, that the assumptions of both East and West must change.

22

F ROM THE GIVING of names — whether as told in Genesis, or as explained in the philosophy of St Augustine — stems the entire mentality of the West. This was the very process of making discrete objects, things that have substance, the atomic bricks composing the world. From this source likewise derives the metaphysical idea of the person: an object apart, having a life and a soul. Indeed, without Adam's capacity to name things, God himself, as the creator of those things, would have been inconceivable.

It was this God that gave a Jew his identity as a person; and it was St Paul's fateful decision that circumcision should not be a requirement of Christianity that loosed Christians to seek their identity as persons wherever they could find it in the world. Hence Timothy's 'circumcision in Christ'. (The medical profession has nowadays somewhat resumed the role of the priesthood in these respects.) One wonders how much homicide might have been avoided in the world had Christians not been allowed this license to establish their personhood. Furthermore, the assumption of separate entities lends credence to the notion of causation: a world of billiard balls is seemingly one ruled by determinable cause and effect. And from this there flows, not so much the laws of science, as the presumption that these laws hold the key to the very reason for our being here.

It is a dearly bought presumption. Perhaps its main cost is to our emotional lives: in the inhibition of touch and physical contact needed to preserve our separateness, and therewith our sense of reality. Drugs, of one kind or another, are the immemorial antidote to the restlessness induced in mankind by its reification of all that exists in the world, including the self, and therewith the endless regression involved in the pursuit of the self in search of the self. Of course, this is the religious exercise, inescapably imposed on us by language.

But, ultimately, there is no rest to be had from the illusions of reification. They contain no certainty in which we can find comfort. Although there is causation,cause and effect are forever uncertain. Yet if uncertainty is the only certainty, then uncertainty must also be uncertain. Certainty must then be possible. This, indeed, is what gives licence to faith. Yet the kind of faith that precludes uncertainty is only for those for whom life without its certainties is unendurable. For such, Nietzche's 'superman' would have nothing but contempt. For him, to accept faith is to settle for a lower order of life. But, compassionately speaking, this faith is not to be scorned, for by our practice of naming things we have contrived a world of monstrous, centralised inflexibilities. Actually to live with uncertainty, and hence with change, requires a flexibility in our forms of life which only smallness of scale can offer. The larger and more centralised our institutions, the more resistant will they be to change — and the more catastrophic will be any change when it comes.

So if 'things' are illusory — mere metaphysical resonances — it must be the case that the world is nothing but relationships. But relationships between what? How can there be relationships without substances? Moreover, if substances are actually only reifications, relationships themselves must lie between concepts, not things. However, that is all that relationships ever were: they never were substantial. It is only by contrast with the pretensions of things to reality that credence adheres to relationships.

But there is another path: one dependent upon neither substances nor relationships. This is to accept that the world is as it is. In Buddhist terms, this is known as 'emptiness' — though, because of the vagaries of language, it is also sometimes known as 'fullness'. Whichever, this path makes sense only by discarding the verb 'to be': which is as much as to say that language describes no reality, and that there is no precedence of being over non-being. So that when one says: 'The world is as it is', one is only getting as near as one can get in words to saying that the dialectic of language is ultimately empty of value. Yet one cannot reach this point without using words to do so.

How austere a doctrine this must seem to be! Even more austere than Stoicism (though hopefully not so sterile). For unlike the Stoic absolutes of duty and honour, the doctrine of emptiness allows of human frailty. It does so because its end is forever out of reach: one can only ever be moving towards it. Effectively, it is non-teleological. So long as there is language, so long will mankind not be at rest; and so long as language is abused (as it will be) and used for what it cannot be made to do, so long will knowledge of the world as it is — enlightenment — be denied to any mortal, even the most saintly among us. Even one rotten apple threatens the barrel: of such is the interdependence, the non-differentiation of the world as it is. Meanwhile, all we can do is keep at it.

But how? What aids to our frailty are there? Perhaps love is one vehicle. Of course, love is meaningless apart from hate — which is not to say that if one loves one must also hate, or be hated. But if there were not hate there would still be that which we call love, because this is what shows us the world, not through our own eyes, not as the self sees it, but through the eyes of others.

And maybe another vehicle, flawed as it has become, is art. Of course, art is arguably just another language and, with its performer and its audience, as dualistic and as corrupted as any other. Perhaps, in its indulgence of the self, art as we know it has gone past the point of no-return, and will never express what the Balinese, who have no word for 'art', imply when they say: 'We do everything as best we can'. Nevertheless, there is no question that art has the power to inspire, that each work of art tells us of the world as it is. If only as an antidote to the debasement of our ordinary discourse, art remains a necessary refuge of the human spirit. Or perhaps it is the shamanism of our times, and is as perrenially indispensable for our entrancement.

When all is said and done, love and art, like language itself, serve only to keep our heads above water while we are gaining the other shore. We need them because it is so improbable that other shore will ever be reached.

23

'LANGUAGE-GAME' IS TO WESTERN THOUGHT what 'emptiness' is to Eastern. Yet far more than that: it has the potential to rescue the Eastern tradition from the morass into which it has fallen. This morass is one of language itself: of using language to say that language cannot be used to say what language cannot say. Even 'emptiness'! For language, and therefore thought, cannot say anything about reality, because concepts are dualistic: they all owe their existence to whatever other concepts they are distinct from. Since thought cannot grasp reality, there has always been a temptation latent in the Eastern mind to opt for some regime of no-thought.

Of course, the thinkers themselves knew better, and said so, but emptiness is a hard concept to grasp — particularly so when it means its opposite — and few have followed matters that far. The consequence, then, has been an abject Eastern vulnerability to materialism. Yet if, by contrast, thought is recognised to be not a statement about reality but a game, then it need not reach its conclusion in some impenetrable paradox. Such a game would equally involve both 'subjective' and 'objective'; it would treat my subjective pain just as it would treat the objective cosmos; and it would therefore accord the self no more reality than language itself allows. Hence this game partakes not of paradox but of everyday life. Whenever thinking can be taken no further, the game finds its conclusion in some form of life.

Yet it may be asked whether the game between words and the world posits 'reality' in some way, much as it is posited by the unrealities of dualistic thought. In the latter case, of course, it leads one logically to the practice of meditation, which can be construed as absorption in the real. In the Western tradition, Trappism, with its rejection of language, would seem to be a parallel path. But it is not so, for what grammar is there in nothing but silence? Without grammar, there can be no meaning to the silence.

In Western logic, then, is there nothing beyond those 'forms of life', whatever they may chance to be? Is there no meaning to the world itself? Well, there is all the grammar of language itself, the element within which humanity is a-swim, and without which no single language-game could be pursued. The totality of all this alone makes possible our grasp of any part of life. And that totality is the whole, not just of our grammar, but of both our grammar and the world, indissolubly so. Thus, in our language games today we speak of the 'environment': it has come to the top of our thoughts, perhaps as a surrogate of that 'reality' we previously sought in the atom. But to treat of the environment as an icon, as an object apart from the game of language, would be fraudulent. Simply as an agent, however, of the indivisibility of the language-animal, man, from the world, the environment is a potent symbol for our times.

In this perspective, 'thinking' about the environment becomes more of a reverie upon it. So, 'what we cannot speak about we must pass over in silence' — yes, but not quiescence! And any such reverie will be aesthetic rather than analytic in character. (Isn't the haiku meditation of a kind?) Could it be that such controlled dreaming amidst all the world's business and all that mysteriously is in it would be a practice more congenial to Westerners than the conventional, detached Eastern forms of meditation? Could such reverie be a more appropriate way of reaching 'beyond' the forms of life to which language leads us, and which, by their very finiteness, would seem to posit some other and boundless form of expression? Silence, perhaps.

The art of such dreaming, existing perhaps as a combination of prayer (words) with meditation (the wordless), would consist in its being both non-egoistic and non-reductionistic about whatever it dwelt upon. It would simply accept — yet be awake. (In fact, do we dream — or are we dreamt?) However, before we raise false hopes about what should anyway be pursued as a kind of therapy — something requisite to health rather than salvation — it needs to be borne in mind that language, by which we differentiate all things, is also all that comprehends us, who use it. So should we not then rest content with this dichotomy? Is it not sufficient that we are comprehended by what we comprehend? Is it possible to be more reverend than that? And, if not, who can tell what might be the product of such fortune?

24

WHEN ONE HAS FINISHED one's work for the day ... well, there's always tomorrow. Tomorrow serves to postpone tomorrow, to put off asking oneself what today has meant. Though perhaps at the end of the week or month, the pay-packet may satisfy that need. And perhaps the pay-packet, and the pension that follows it, may indefinitely satisfy one as to what the days have meant. 'Tomorrow and tomorrow and tomorrow...'

It is important not to pause over the pay-packet to consider what it means. (Just asking for more will help postpone that temptation.) Yet one can be caught out — just as one can with all other means of passing the time. Yet the reason jobs matter so much more than those other activities is that they pass the time so much better than anything else; they disguise boredom far better. They do this, surely, because of the wide agreement amongst us that our job measures our worth. Well, it used to be so agreed. But in recent years millions upon millions have been unemployed with scarcely a political ripple being caused. This would suggest that disillusion about a job as a measure of worth has been spreading. So we have been caught out by people not being caught out: by wrong expectations of others' expectations. Still, this is but indicative of the lurking question, always waiting to catch us out, as to what the day's work has meant, or simply the meaning of our job.

Nevertheless, it is still comparatively rare for that question to be asked by someone of their own accord, rather than its being posed by outside forces. Only the rich seem to do this of themselves—though increasingly often. It is not a question that could even arise if one's job were infused with some meaning other than the pay-packet; but then it would not be a job, but a vocation. (How satisfying to have a vocation! How independent of social standards! How existential!) It is a longing anyone might have who ever allowed a hint of that question about the day's work to enter their heads. Yet how dangerous it could be if we all had a vocation! For then we should all be asking one another questions about what our vocations meant — and we should not know how to answer them intelligently. There is certainly not the same measure of agreement about vocations as there is about jobs. It would end in bafflement. So should the questions not be asked? Shouldn't we just go back to our benign, if mindless, employment?

But questions will ask themselves, and perhaps that is why people are leaving the crowded concourses of our cities: so that, free of the oppressive conformity of numbers, self-knowledge might be better pursued. What matters, then, is what happens when each and every one of us recognises our ignorance, as indeed we must. For any questioning of the sort here in mind can only end in silence. One reaches the bounds of what can be said: the explanations of what one's work means, one's way of life, end in a vacuum. And the mere prospect of this is frightening. (It is perhaps why so much work nowadays is performed to the blare of canned music.) Better, some may think, to endure the anomie of the city: to sit for hours each day encapsulated in one's car in a crawl of traffic, or underground crammed next to people with whom one has precisely not the slightest relationship, assaulted by advertisements from which one has no escape except by closing one's eyes, part of a meaningless busy-ness. Oh, Lethe!

But the evidence is to the contrary: people have tried urban amnesia and want out of it. So how is the silence to be endured? Why, by listening to it! But not by listening to the silence within oneself: rather, by listening to the silence of others. Listening to others' silence, that is what makes community. In the chatter of the city, however, there is never the possibility of any such silence falling: thus we cannot share our silence there, nor can there by any community. There are, of course, manifold professional 'communities', or communities of some common purpose, but all these are of their nature exclusive. The only communities that can embrace our common humanity are those of silence, of one another's silence.

And, for these to exist, they must be both small and themselves belong in the natural world. For the silence to which we must come is also the silence of all that is speechless. We ourselves cannot be silent if we cannot hear the non-speech of the world, as the bird does not know the air, nor the fish feel water, nor fire burn fire.

25

WORDS CANNOT REFER to objects, because there are no objects for them to refer to. Objects derive their identity only from their not being referred to by other words. So if logically words do not refer even to words, so that the only reality is 'emptiness' (as Nagarjuna demonstrated two millenia back), one might be forgiven for supposing that such a truly rigorous philosophy — as opposed to that illusory optimism, all those footnotes to Plato, with which the West has always been fobbed off — does not hold out the prospect of much joy in life.

Of course your enlightened individual, who has arrived at an ineffable and ecstatic silence, would be an exception to this conclusion. And even anyone claiming to have had Shamanistic out-of-body experiences or mystic flights might also not quarrel with philosophy thus construed. To take, however, the, nearest example that comes to mind of someone who in himself embodied all these verities — namely Wittgenstein — his life at first glance would scarcely be an advertisement to a generally self-indulgent public of the merits of such a rigorous philosophy.

It is not just the self-imposed austerities of his life that would make it difficult to commend his example but, to be frank, the high moral tone that could exalt Beethoven yet denigrate Shakespeare as being altogether too down-to-earth would, even for a nigh-idolatrous admirer, be a little hard to accept. It is almost as if the Christian-Platonic association of matter with evil was being let in again by the back door. Yet remember that Wittgenstein's reported last words were: 'Tell them it's been wonderful.' One can't think that this was just a statement of the joys of masochism.

So is there any hope for the lovers of cakes and ale? Well, what if a huge detour has been made in search of higher things by those who have renounced their taste for cakes and ale? And what if that detour has brought them back to their starting point, to where the lovers of cakes and ale have always been? Logically, alas, this would be to associate Chartres, say, with the bloated metaphysics of the Christianising of Aristotle in the middle ages. But should we baulk at even so presumptuous a possibility?

After all, however exalted Chartres may be, has it not lost the womb-like mystery of the Romanesque it super-seded, and which was of the scale of everyman? Perhaps the builders of Chartres, the labourers, did actually wor-ship there, but no longer would they do so. The supposed glories of our culture, whether Beethoven or Shakespeare, are now all one, or rather zero, to 90% of the population. The gap is immense between their daily lives, in the grip of materialism, and anything touched by even the ves-tiges of high culture. Is it possible then, in a manner of speaking, to maintain that Chartres is responsible for this?

Entirely so, it seems to me. Without 'art' there is no vulgarity. And 'art' is what we've got: as much beyond the reach and concern of most people as the soaring meta-physics of St Thomas Aquinas. Of course, Chartres itself is actually grounded in the labyrinth inscribed on its floor: a residual but overlooked contact with the mysteries of a much more ancient culture. But if one wonders why our culture left the ground, and why it had to be expressed for all eternity in stone (whereas, for comparison, the holiest shrine of Shinto in Japan is deliberately destroyed and rebuilt every twenty years), perhaps the explanation can be found encoded in the concept of causation, and hence in that of creation? Such notions can be traced back at least as far as Plato — even though, conversely, Nagarjuna, on the other side of the world, was at pains to refute them?

Of course, creation myths are harmless enough pro-vided we do not let ourselves be bewitched by them. Yet one does wonder whether our pervasive prudery has not been fed on the sickly premise that it was when Adam and

Eve knew their nakedness, i.e. their sinfulness, that they clothed themselves, rather than when they clothed themselves, for good practical reasons, that they thus knew their nakedness. (One hears that there are 'willie bars' in Tokyo, where men, doubtless in Western suits, go of an evening simply to expose their genitals harmlessly. Is this their revenge on Western values?) At all events, the notion of causation carries with it a temptation, not just to presume some first cause, but to reify the manifold substances of which it is compounded. Causation likewise permits of repetition and hence also the reversibility of time, although not of entropy and nothingness.

Once Aristotle had been rediscovered in the twelfth century and the idea of measurement (if only of how many angels could stand on the head of a pin) had been incorporated into Christian metaphysics, a course was set that was bound to leave everyday life behind. Whitehead, in our own century, called this 'the fallacy of misplaced concreteness': meaning that the more we abstract particular causes and effects from their amorphous contextual complexity, the more intractible become the difficulties by which we find ourselves beset. (What is the story of our civilisation but of its twists and turns to escape from the concrete in which Christianity was set at Nicea?) Nowadays, no doubt, Whitehead would have talked about the environment. Indeed, the contemporary concern for the environment, even if it is little more than a reaction against our all-pervasive, dour instrumentalism, is a sign of hope that there might still be joy in life.

Maybe environmentalism isn't the view of life we associate with the lovers of cakes and ale, but this is surely because so much of contemporary environmentalism is really disguised self-interest. Perhaps it is also because the lovers of cakes and ale themselves have been debased into grabbing whatever they can get in the market-place, rather than sharing their enjoyment of life with others. Even so, to have an organic view of life, which is what the environment implies (and is what Whitehead was on about), is actually compatible with that most rigorous philosophy which leads to silence in the face both of things and of language.

Its premise, for one thing, is harmony, rather than causation, and hence the precedence of the aesthetic over the moral, which is a by-product of causation. But, perhaps more profoundly, the origins of that silence lie in the dismissal of the separation, and hence the identity, of things as things. That rejection is a rejoicing in the unity of whatever is real. And it is the unique contribution of Wittgenstein that, having himself taken the Western atomistic premise of causation to its uttermost limits, he clawed himself back, if not all the way to the point of departure of that cul-de-sac, yet quite far enough to bring the alternative route in sight.

He did so, not by ever more sophisticated philosophising, but by means of a game: the game of language. Of course, we think of a game as somehow not 'real'. But since reality itself is under question in our newly rigorous philosophy, at least nothing can be lost by approaching it through games. The very point about a game is that it makes sense through the context in which it is played, through the 'form of life', in Wittgenstein's terms, to which its rules are adapted. It is this context, this environment, that provides the reality of everyday life, and which cannot itself be reduced to the character of some one thing.

Perhaps this reality is only an enchantment, but it is all that most of us can hope to enjoy. It bespeaks a situation in which all the uncertainties of a game are sustainable. Moreover, it proclaims radically different values from those by which we are now governed: values, for instance, of co-operation rather than competition. Equally radically, it suggests different social structures, starting with the dismantling of the nation state and all other forms of gigantism, and ending with the restoration of community. And, furthermore, it allows those values to be incorporated into our understanding of reality, such that the

75

material and the spiritual, or the empirical and the moral, are not treated as distinct compartments. It thereby liberates us from literalism. Nor would art then be separate from everyday life, which would then be a continual ceremony.

It is admittedly an agenda for a thousand years, but also one for starting now.

26

THE DEAD DO NOT mourn themselves. In life also we are what others perceive us to be. Hence, a person's own life is like a protracted speech in a private language — which of itself is unreal. Thus the notion of 'a life', *in vacuo*, takes on the character of a dream, such that all our waking is but a continuation of dreaming. Perhaps, then, we do not have to sleep to dream, but rather our dreaming periodically becomes so powerful that it breaks through the membrane of sleep and into the world? When (and if) this happens, would we not stand in need of language, if only to harness our dreams? (Death, then, *pace* Hamlet, is but dreamlessness?). At any rate, waking and sleeping, consciousness and unconsciousness, cannot be taken as different realms of reality, governed by different laws. Insofar as waking calls forth language and language removes us from 'reality', sleep is arguably closer to whatever reality is. Sleep is our natural, if chaotic, state. As long as we draw the conclusion that we must dedicate our life to a reality that is unknowable, such ideas as these are in no way nihilistic. If we accept them, then not pride, but humility, would condition our actions, and the overmighty, the hyper-conscious would be brought low.

Yet all this is but a metaphysics of 'the person' and, if not in the superficial West, it, along with the metaphysics of time and substance, has long since been vainly debated in the Buddhist East two thousand or more years ago by followers of the Abidharma, and been brought to earth by Nagarjuna. There is nothing new under the sun: the West has still to learn how true that is. Nevertheless, each new generation must learn for itself that it is bewitched by the dualism of self and world, and by the overpowering sense which language brings with it of the immensity by which the self is surrounded, and so made to seem real. And woe betide any generation that does not do so! Its resultant pride in its dominion will lead to its fall. In our traffic with the world, this renewal is ultimately inescapable — it is what we are so painfully passing through nowadays: as inescapable as sleep and silence.

So what is a life but another tension between the non-dualistic and the dualistic? between knowing the truth and an inability to accept it? Given such a dichotomy, either all our propositions, all that constitutes 'the world', would, as Wittgenstein said, be accidental and our values without foundation; alternatively, all that is is but of the stuff of dreams. But if what we think of as a life is what mediates these apparent alternatives — as it might also mediate time present and time passing — in practice, how is this to be done?

It must depend on whether life is understood as a gift, or whether we have it, so to speak, on credit as a debt; and the suffering inescapable in life suggests it can only be a debt. But is it a debt that can ever be paid? The consequences of whatever one does will never end, just as one is a consequence of all that has ever happened. (They tell us we will each, at some time, most probably incorporate in our bodies a molecule or two that once was part of Socrates or Jesus Christ.) So language instils in us the 'instinct' of guilt: that our actions must be accounted for to repay this debt for our life. Mountains of morality are constructed from this bewitchment by language — and perhaps necessarily so (up to a point) if day by day the good is to be distinguished from the bad. Nevertheless, this is no assurance that the debt is such that it can ever be redeemed.

Although language (the house we live in) orders the world, it has nothing to do with the elements outside that beat upon our senses. It pretends to do so, of course, but just look at what happens when the provision language has made for our guilt — hell — is destructured! Violence invades our quietist streets, and drugs make free of our bodies. Heaven, also, then dissolves into Marks and Spencer. And, though we may pay our debts to 'M & S', yet even they would lay no claim to immortality.

Nevertheless, we are tempted to take shelter from death in materialism, for (though it may lack a certain nobility) we still imagine we can thus repay the debt we owe for our lives. We believe that we can somehow cash in our debt by giving our lives to expiate our (and even others') sins. But it is the debt that survives, not ourselves. For there is no life to be given.

27

'**B** UT,' ASKED MY INDIAN FRIEND, 'what about Advaita? Is that not also non-dualism, the divine ground of all things, including God, which subsumes all positives and negatives. *Neti, Neti* — not this, not this: all that is not is not what is: which is Brahman.'

So I might, after all, be able to credit God without doing violence thereby to the integrity of my mind? Then I could release my imagination to enjoy all the riches, all the wonderful structures of our kind of civilisation, all that we have wrested responsibly and considerately from the earth, our mother? What a relief, then, to be able to choose between nihilism and idealism (to choose idealism, of

course) and not be confined to the middle way! To rejoin
the mainstream of mankind!

Yet, if there is Brahman, is there not also not-Brah-
man? Is not this reduction of things to one thing, in this
case a kind of super-substance that accounts for all others, logically infinite? And are not all things then necessarily but reifications, mental constructs? And do we not
stop at Brahman only because it suits us so to do? And
if we stop at that stage, why should this be other than,
for some reason, to keep 'things' as they are? The caste
system, for instance. Or take the analogous case of the
great medieval Christian mystics: Meister Eckhart, for
instance, 'I pray to God to rid me of God'; and the un-
known author of the *Cloud of Unknowing*, 'The most
godly way of knowing is knowing by unknowing'. They
also sought the 'god-ground', the Godhead. However,
though Eckhart was arrested for heresy by the inquisition (yet mercifully died of natural causes), he protested
— and with sound reason — his fidelity to the Church.
He wanted to purify it, not to destroy it — though he
was surely naive about its secular, political dimension.

For these mystics were children of the metaphysics
whereby Thomas Aquinas had transcended the challenge
of the newly rediscovered empiricism of Aristotle. Their
thoughts stemmed from the same perplexed impulse as
sent the crusaders on their shameful way. The Church
remained the necessary vehicle for interpreting God to
man, implicitly thereby both affirming God's creation and
man's stewardship of it, and hence mankind's privileged
apartness from it. Indeed, can mankind ever escape the
trappings of the metaphysical, the reification of things?
Even a mankind that learns from quantum mechanics
that maybe there are only relationships, not things, or
that the notion of causation posited by the existence of
things is an illusion? Is not the sheer uncertainty of non-
dualism, the not-knowing of cause and effect, humanly
unendurable?

And how could uncertainty be our God? Isn't this, in

fact, what Buddhists mean by emptiness? Surely the given certainties of metaphysics are easier to live with, demanding as they do only belief! Moreover, is this not why, historically, Buddhism, which alone is rigorously non-dualistic (and therefore a-theistic), has either survived only as a monastic culture — a kind of a-theocracy — or else in conjunction with another 'religion' such as Shinto, or by edicts of the likes of an Emperor Ashoka? And is this not why it has periodically suffered its own lapses into metaphysics?

Perhaps language imprints upon us an overwhelming illusion of the reality it so assuredly describes, and will always tempt us into what actually it can never serve to communicate — truth or beauty, for instance. If so, it is a sad prospect. For it would mean that, *pace* Darwin, mankind is a uniquely self-destructive species. Between the Vedic Advaita (or equally the god-ground of Eckhart, also striving nobly to escape the structural constraints of its culture) and the rigorous but universal non-dualism of Nagarjuna, there may seem to some only a hair's-breadth of difference. But, logically, this is as great as the difference between classical physics and quantum mechanics, or between post- and pre-Augustine Christianity. It is a hairline crack that allows metaphysics to seep in. It allows us, for instance, to reify even the environment and then to subject it to the stewardship of our contending, but equally metaphysical selves.

'Why do the nations so furiously rage together,
And the people imagine a vain thing?'

Why, indeed, other than because ironically they are under the spell, not so much of Jehovah, as of their dread of silence. That's why there is no harder discipline than meditation.

28

S O, AFTER ALL, what is a life? Which is as much as to
say, why do we ask this question? For of itself a life
is less than nothing: scarcely even a manner of speech,
of neither substance, nor time. There is no continuity to
it and nothing about it but what is accidental. We speak
of 'my life' as if that defined, for all its transient over-
tones, something of truth: and yet this self that is thus
defined is but a convenient fiction. And though the
mourners shall go about the streets, yet that which is
ended would not have ended had it not begun; and ending and beginning, sorrow and joy, only lend each other
the cloak of reality. To speak of 'a life' is only to play a
language game. But that is not to say why we should
play this game at all. Why, then, should this particular
end and this beginning be so significant? Why else than
because a life is an affirmation that the world is as it
is? A life defies the apparent inexorabilities of matter,
time and corruption. It is the ultimate symbol — a symbol that represents itself — signifying that reality
neither is nor is not. And this is a mystery.

ENVOI

You are my hillsides and their hedgerows,
My pastures and the red soil beneath them;
The cross-roads at some time-haunted place;
The solitude of wetlands shared with birds.
You are my clouds, washing the always unimaginable
    blue,
My garden trees: that olive with its second lease
Of life, the ilex that's my winter's grace;
My evenings with their sea-calm quietness.
You are my Mediterranean,
And my grey homeland: my room, my town;
All my fond hopes, and sometimes their disgrace;
The celebrations of us mortals down the years.
    These shall all change to yours when I am gone,
    To husband them, as I have with my tears.